SACRED PATTERNS

WORK, REST, AND PLAY
IN A JOYFUL VISION OF LIFE

RICK HOWE

BOOKS BY RICK HOWE

Path of Life: Finding the Joy You've Always Longed For, 2012, University Ministries Press Revised Edition, 2017. 279 pages.

River of Delights: Quenching Your Thirst For Joy, Volume 1, 2015, University Ministries Press Revised Edition, 2017. 230 pages.

River of Delights: Quenching Your Thirst For Joy, Volume 2, 2015, University Ministries Press Revised Edition, 2017. 250 pages.

Living Waters: Daily Refreshment for Joyful Living, 2017, University Ministries Press. 393 pages.

Reasons of the Heart: Joy and the Rationality of Faith, 2017, University Ministries Press. 250 pages.

FOR SMALL GROUP STUDIES

Enjoying God: Discovering the Greatest of All Pleasures, University Ministries Press, 2017. 122 pages.

Love's Delights: The Joys of Marriage and Family, University Ministries Press, 2017. 104 pages.

Sacred Patterns: Work, Rest, and Play in a Joyful Vision of Life, University Ministries Press, 2017. 122 pages.

Kingdom Manifesto: A Call to Joyful Activism, University Ministries Press, 2017. 104 pages.

Joy and the Problem of Evil, University Ministries Press, Boulder, 2017. 122 pages.

For more information, visit www.rickhowe.org.

UNIVERSITY MINISTRIES PRESS

BOULDER, COLORADO

Copyright © 2015.

University Ministries Press Edition, 2017.

ISBN: 978-0-9962696-3-6

CONTENTS

AUTHOR'S NOTE

The material in *Sacred Patterns* is taken from my book, *River of Delights: Quenching Your Thirst For Joy, Volume 2.* I thought it would be worthwhile to take these very important dimensions of our lives – work, rest, and play – and put them in one place for readers who wish to explore these very important topics in their own right.

As you will see, there are many endnotes. If texts of Scripture are not given in full in the main body of a chapter, they have been included in the endnotes to make it possible for you to read the book without the extra chore of looking them up yourself. There are also many references to other works, as well as my own comments. My suggestion is that you read *Sacred Patterns* first without interacting with the endnotes to trace the flow of thought without interruption, and then read it again with those references.

The "Questions for Thought and Discussion" for each chapter reflect my hope that you will study this book with others, my belief that learning in community is the best way to learn, and my prayer that God will use this book to create communities of joy for the advancement of his Kingdom.

PREFACE

An apocalyptic foreboding has many in its grip, strengthened by endless newsfeeds and broadcasts featuring economic woes, violence, terrorism, wars and threats of war, corruption in high places, depletion of energy resources, global climate change, natural catastrophes, pestilence, and toxins in our environment and our food.

No wonder words like *anxiety, depression, melancholy,* and *stress* are used to describe our generation! Historians in the future might well call ours *The Age of Prozac*. Depressive disorders are widespread. The pharmaceutical industry has grown rich on them.

The fact that this emotional epidemic grows unabated should signal the possibility that we have misdiagnosed and mistreated the problem. I don't deny that there are frightening factors behind our personal angst and cultural malaise, but I believe that there is an underlying cause that we ignore at our own greater peril. We are disoriented and dysfunctional. We are disoriented because we have removed God from our vision of life, and dysfunctional because we vainly attempt to live without him. Much else (economic woes, violence, toxins in our environment, et al) results directly or indirectly from this.

"A joyful heart is a good medicine."[1] This was once proverbial wisdom. It is true because joy connects us with God, and that is the healthiest place for us to be. Dallas Willard wrote, "Full joy is our first line of defense against weakness, failure, and disease of mind and body."[2] Peter Kreeft says much the same: "A joyful spirit inspires joyful feelings and even a more psychosomatically healthy body. (For example, we need less sleep when we have joy and have more resistance to all kinds of diseases from colds to cancers.)"[3] This ancient wisdom deserves a revival in our day. In fact, it is our only hope.

The premises of this book are that joy links us with God, it can touch and transform every dimension of our lives, including our work, our rest, and our play, and we will flourish only as we position ourselves to receive this gift from Him. Read on to discover how!

CHAPTER 1

JOY AT WORK: CREATION

As this book is being written, economies are in a downward spiral. Bankruptcies and foreclosures are as thick as ants on a piece of cake left behind in a park. Many people are without jobs. Many have lost savings, retirement portfolios, funding for college, health insurance, and the ability to make it from one paycheck to the next. The recession is nearly as wide as the world.

You would never hire me as an economist, so I won't venture into that domain. But if I understand anything of God's design for work in the Scriptures, I can only say that our economic illness, at its deepest, is spiritual in nature. We have lost our way, and with every step we wander farther from the path. The pathway is God's purposes for work. Not just my job or yours, but work itself. Human labor in a larger vision of life.

THE GENESIS OF WORK

"In the beginning God created." These words make all the difference in the world because they tell us that the world has a Maker. It was planned. Designed. Our stories have a place in God's Story, and work is an important part of the tale. If there is one God who created the world and all that is in it, then everything in the world finds meaning in relation to him.[1] There is no other way that it could be. Everything – birth, life, death, work, play, love, marriage, families, cities, and nations – is meaningful in the design and purposes of our Creator.

If there is one God who is the Maker of all things, the distinctions we create and impose on the world may amuse him, but they are not informative to him. Everything in creation belongs to him. All things – from the dance of sub-atomic particles to the migration of stars – serve his purposes. We might distinguish between sacred and secular, public and private, and church and state, but these distinctions easily mislead us, and they are irrelevant to God. There is one domain in the universe, and it is his. We will find the meaning and purpose of work here, or it will not be found at all.

God, joy, and work. The link between joy and work begins with God himself. He takes boundless pleasure in his creative endeavors. The Psalmist exclaimed: "May the glory of the LORD endure forever, may the LORD rejoice in His works!"[2] It will; he does. In the inspired narrative of creation, "And God saw that it was good," is a commentary on God's pleasure in his handiwork. Nicholas Wolterstoff has written: "This world in which we live is an artifact brought into being by God. It represents a success on the part of God – God who is love – not a failure. In contemplation of what he had made God found delight. . . . God pronounced His "Yes" upon it all, a "Yes" of delight and love."[3]

The Sabbath celebrates the fact that God ceased from his original work of creation. But his work of giving and sustaining life continues to this day:

> O LORD, how manifold are your works!
>> In wisdom have you made them all;
>> the earth is full of your creatures.

When you send forth your Spirit, they are created;
and you renew the face of the ground. (Psalm 104:24, 30)[4]

In ways that only he knows and angels glimpse, God continues to work in the universe he made: "Jesus answered them, 'My Father is working until now, and I am working.'"[5] If God stopped working, the earth would stop spinning. The sun would stop shining. Clouds would stop raining. Plants would stop growing. Our hearts would stop beating. Our minds would stop thinking. More than we can imagine depends upon God's boundless joy in his endless work. These are the headwaters of our joy in work. Ours is sourced in his.

The *imago Dei*. The most fundamental truth about us is that we have been made in the image of God.[6] We were created to mirror him in the world. There are several facets to the reflection.[7] Before sin entered the world, it included a reflection of God's moral beauty. The likeness was unsullied. Even now, like God, we are rational, affective, volitional beings. Our abilities to think, love, make decisions and act as agents in the world are grounded in our likeness to God. Like him, we are relational: We were made to share life with others. Like him, we are creative: We can imagine something and bring it about. Like God, we work.[8]

Work in the Garden. Eden was God's handiwork, but it was also work for the hands of our first parents.[9] The One who named every star in the night sky[10] delegated the task of naming Eden's creatures to Adam:

> Now out of the ground the LORD God had formed every beast of the field and every bird of the heavens and brought them to the man to see what he would call them. And whatever the man called every living creature, that was its name. The man gave names to all livestock and to the birds of the heavens and to every beast of the field. (Genesis 2:19-20)

Creating a taxonomy and nomenclature for the animal kingdom is work.[11] The God who brought these creatures into being could have named them, as well. That he assigned this task to Adam signals the significance of human work from the beginning. We see it again in Adam's stewardship of the Garden. His charge was to "work it and keep it."[12] The God who created the Garden could have cultivated and kept it, as well, but he honors us by sharing his work with us.

Our cultural mandate. God wants us to work. But what does he want us to do with our work? What is the aim of our labor? What purpose is it meant to serve? Theologians find the answer to these questions in what they call the "cultural mandate" given to us at the beginning of our story. We find the directive in these words:

> Then God said, 'Let us make man in our image, after our likeness. And let them have dominion over the fish of the sea and over the birds of the havens and over the livestock and over al the earth and over every creeping thing that creeps on the earth.' (Genesis 1:26)

> So God created man in his own image,
> in the image of God he created him;
> male and female he created them. (Genesis 1:27)

> And God blessed them. And God said to them, 'Be fruitful and multiply and fill the earth and subdue it, and have dominion over the fish of the sea and over the birds of the heavens and over every living thing that moves on the earth.' (Genesis 1:28)

The world is not ours; it is God's.[13] We are not owners; we are managers. An important part of what it means to be made in God's image lies in the charge to rule and steward the earth in God's stead, fulfilling his vision for this planet and the human project.[14] Psalm 8 echoes the creation narrative:

O LORD, our Lord,
    how majestic is your name in all the earth!
You have set your glory above the heavens. . . .
When I look at your heavens, the work of your fingers,
    the moon and the stars, which you have set in place,
what is man that you are mindful of him,
    and the son of man that you care for him?
Yet you have made him a little lower than the heavenly beings
and crowned him with glory and honor.
You have given him dominion over the works of your hands;
    you have put all things under his feet,
 all sheep and oxen,
    and also the beasts of the field,
the birds of the heavens, and the fish of the sea,
    whatever passes along the paths of the seas.
 O LORD, our Lord,
    how majestic is your name in all the earth!

We obey this mandate from the Creator when we discover resources and develop the potential he put into his world, when we harness all things for his glory and the good of humanity, and when we do it in a way that honors, protects, and preserves the world he made and has entrusted to us.

The cultural mandate is meant to form and inform all human labor. Work is designed to be about something much bigger and more important than the discrete tasks that bring us a paycheck. There is pleasure in doing any job well, but there is a greater joy when our work displays the *imago Dei* and fulfills its mandate to bring about God's purposes for our world.

Goodness, beauty, and truth. The ancient Greeks saw goodness, beauty, and truth as pure, transcendent realities that shape our experience in the world.[15] Whatever we find to be good in our world is an instance of the Good, which is timeless and supreme. The beautiful in our experience participates in Beauty, above and beyond our sentience. Whatever is true is grounded in absolute, eternal, and unchanging Truth. Augustine and other early Christian thinkers embraced this, but taught that God is the transcendent Source of all goodness, beauty, and truth. They are united and exist eternally in him.[16]

The people of faith whose stories are chronicled in the Bible didn't think about these things abstractly (or if they did, they didn't leave us a record of their thoughts). But if you had asked them if God is good, they would have said, "Taste and see!"[17] If you asked if God is beautiful, they would have said, "Breathtakingly!" And if you had asked them if God is truthful, they would have exclaimed, "Absolutely!" If you had asked them how they knew these things, they wouldn't have constructed a chain of reasoning to get them to those conclusions, they would have talked about God's gracious self-disclosure and their matching experience in worship and life.

To say that God is good is to say that he is supremely worthy, supremely valuable, supremely desirable. It is also to say that he is supremely beneficent. He the Source of all good things in the world. He seeks our well-being. He desires to see us flourish in life. The commands he gives reflect his character. They are grounded in his goodness.

To say that God is beautiful is to say that he is to the worshiping heart what color, shape and texture are to aesthetic experience. Encountering God in worship brings the same kind of pleasure as gazing in appreciation and awe at a sunset – only infinitely better. It is more than this, however. To say that God is beautiful is also to affirm that all beauty in the world comes from him.

To say that God is true is to say first that he is unwaveringly faithful to himself. "If we are faithless, he remains faithful – for he cannot deny himself."[18] Everything else in the universe finds its measure in relation to him and his utter truthfulness. All that he discloses about himself and his world fits. It is rock solid. It can be depended on. It can't be any other way, because God can't be any other way (or he would cease to be God, which is impossible).[19] You can lean the full weight of your concern for truth on him. You can believe him. You can trust him in your quest for truth. He is the Source of all truth. If it is true, it is his.

Goodness, beauty, and truth are united in our Creator. They are treasures from him and portals to him. They are structural to the world that he intends for us. They are meant to shape and inform all that we do as his image-bearers. They are essential to the mandate he has given us and are central to our joy. In every endeavor we should ask, "Does this reflect the goodness of God, and his commitment to the well-being of all people? Does it reflect God's commitment to beauty in the world? Does it align with what God has revealed to be true about himself, our world, and the nature and purpose of human life?"

If our cultural mandate were put into a global mission statement, it would look something like this:

> ➤ Vision: to become a fully developed world in harmony with God and his purposes.

> ➤ Mission: to steward the resources of the world for the glory of God and the good of all.

> ➤ Core Values: goodness, beauty, and truth.

> ➤ Intended Outcome: Global joy.

Can you imagine a world in which all endeavors seek to bring this vision about? A world in which all projects are harnessed to this mission? A world in which all enterprises are shaped by these foundational values? A world that flourishes in joy as a result? Perhaps not. We are so very far from this in our fallen condition that these words may seem like a foreign language. It is to the Fall and its impact on work that we must turn.

QUESTIONS FOR THOUGHT AND DISCUSSION

1. Talk about God as a worker, the created world as his work, and his pronouncement that his work is "good." If this is our starting point in understanding work, what difference does it make?

2. How did you understand the image of God before reading this chapter? How does work now fit into your view?

3. How does the "cultural mandate" in Genesis 1:27-28 influence the way you view your work? How does your work fulfill this mandate?

4. Talk about goodness, beauty, and truth, how they relate to God, and how they should shape our activity in the world.

5. Talk about the following "global mission statement for human labor" in terms of your own work, as well as the way our culture approaches work.

   ➤ Vision: to become a fully developed world in harmony with God and his purposes.

   ➤ Mission: to steward the resources of the world for the glory of God and the good of all.

➢ Core Values: goodness, beauty, and truth.

➢ Intended Outcome: Global joy.

CHAPTER 2

JOY AT WORK: FALL

Work is not a punishment. It is not a penalty imposed upon us because of the Fall.[1] Nevertheless, work has been diminished and distorted by the incursion of sin into the world. Sin has destroyed delicate balances and relationships in every dimension of life. It has not only brought alienation with God, it has ruptured human relationships, and broken the harmony between humans and our natural environment. There are thistles and thorns where once there was a Garden. There is sweat on our brows instead of joy in our hearts. There is pain in our labor instead of pleasure in our tasks. It began here:

And to Adam he said,

> "Because you have listened to the voice of your wife
> and have eaten of the tree
> of which I commanded you,
> 'You shall not eat of it,'
> cursed is the ground because of you;
> in pain you shall eat of it all the days of your life;
> thorns and thistles it shall bring forth for you;
> and you shall eat the plants of the field.

> By the sweat of your face you shall eat bread,
> till you return to the ground. (Genesis 3:17-19)

The Fall and the course of history have created powerful forces arrayed against joy in our work. There is a spiritual web of deceit in our fallen world that ensnares all who come near, a predator within whose sting is lethal, and a lair littered with bones beyond numbering.[2]

Practical materialism. This is one thread in hell's web of deceit. It seeks to live as if there were no God. Its philosophical version holds that ours is a physical, mechanistic world. There is matter and motion and nothing more. There is no transcendent spiritual reality. No personal existence beyond the final beat of a heart. Practical materialists may not openly espouse this view, but they live as if it were true. Life, as they see it, will end with their last breath. Until that final and fatal event, their controlling values are governed by physical, tangible interests and concerns: health, wealth, leisure and its many toys, and pleasure and its many possibilities. It's what they talk about at the water cooler, over a meal in a restaurant, a beer at a bar, or tailgating before a football game with their friends.

How does this vision of life play out in the way one approaches work? Goodness, beauty, and truth are replaced by power, profit, and pleasure. Serving others is supplanted by personal survival and success. The glory of God is pushed aside to make room for material interests and concerns. What cannot be measured has no meaning. What cannot be manipulated serves no practical purpose. Work may be useful, but there is nothing transcendent or noble about it. We may pretend otherwise, but there is no ultimate difference between creating a strategic plan for a company, eating in its cafeteria, or relieving oneself in its restrooms. It's all physical. It's all material. Eventually it will all come to the same end.

If materialism is true, life is ultimately about a number of heartbeats and the pleasures and pains that shape life until the final surge of blood flows through our veins. If materialism is true, we would be unwise not to work to gain the best the physical world can offer. We should work to accumulate wealth to sustain and enrich our material life until we draw our last breath. An investment portfolio for a retirement filled with material comforts and pleasures should be one of our loftiest goals.

But if materialism is false, living as if it were true is the height of folly:

> [Jesus] told them a parable, saying, "The land of a rich man produced plentifully, and he thought to himself, 'What shall I do, for I have nowhere to store my crops?' And he said, 'I will do this: I will tear down my barns and build larger ones, and there I will store all my grain and my goods. And I will say to my soul, "Soul, you have ample goods laid up for many years; relax, eat, drink, be merry."' But God said to him, "You fool! This very night your life will be demanded from you. Then who will get what you have prepared for yourself? This is how it will be for anyone who stores up things for themselves but is not rich toward God." And he said to his disciples, "Therefore I tell you, do not be anxious about your life, what you will eat, nor about your body, what you will put on. For life is more than food, and the body more than clothing. (Luke 12:16-23)[3]

The foolishness of practical materialism is not only that it fails to account for an afterlife, it is folly for this life. It prizes false riches, and squanders and neglects true wealth. Its goal becomes a gaol. Wherever it rules, the workplace becomes a battlefield, with material goods and riches the spoils. The powerful exploit the weak; the weak resent the powerful. The wealthy hoard; the poor envy. And all of this for things that will end in graveyards (if materialism is true) and landfills (even if it is not).

Ethical egoism. This is another strand in the hellish web of deceit. It is the antithesis of a vision of work as an endeavor that serves the glory of God and the good of others. Many approach life and work with the guiding principle that everything they do should promote or protect their own interests. If they are prudent, they understand that to get what they want they must get it from others who are seeking what they want. So they compete because they must, cooperate when they must, feign care if they must, and do it all with the calculus of self-interest.[4]

Of course, if everyone lived consistently as an ethical egoist without constraint there would be chaos, with each person's interests pitted against those of everyone else. The social world would be red in tooth and claw,[5] ruled by the laws of the jungle. To prevent this outcome, some sort of social contract is needed to provide order and rules for competition. And there must be a way to enforce the contract: coercive authority. Those who have little want a large, strong government that restrains the self-interest of the rich and powerful. Those who have wealth and power want as little government as possible, or a malleable government that can be shaped to their interests and concerns. Both sides of the economic and political spectrums see each other as mortal enemies.

That our world looks much like this is evidence that many have embraced this vision of life. That some can protest means either that we are the weak who will fall in battle and should be pitied, or that we have glimpsed something greater. Something higher, truer, nobler. Something worth the protest. Something worthy of our pursuit.

Ethical egoism as a way of life destroys the relational dimension of the image of God in us. We were created to live in meaningful relationships characterized by shared interests, concerns, and a commitment to help each other live well. For the ethical egoist, the value of others can only be instrumental. They are means to my ends, and never more than that.

When ethical egoism goes to work, what kind of workplace does it create? In God's wisdom, work is meant to benefit others. It is meant to create a habitat in which all humans flourish. Ethical egoism cares nothing for this. "It's all about me, and it's me against the world." Competitors are not just those who offer a similar product or service in the marketplace, but everyone I work with. They could get the promotion that I want. They could get a bonus while I stare into empty hands. They could get up for work tomorrow while I apply for unemployment benefits and look for another job.

As soon as ethical egoists step into a world with others, they have two options to achieve their ends: force or duplicity.[6] If you have the power to assert your will over others, you might succeed in getting what you want. If you lack that power (and that's most of us), you must be duplicitous. It begins with a double standard. You must treat others as means to your ends, but you don't want them to do the same to you. If you are an egoist, you want everyone else to be an altruist. You want them to have your good in mind, even though you don't have theirs in yours.

If you are an ethical egoist, you must persuade others that you have their interests at heart, when, in fact, you have only your own. You will have to use them without letting them know that you are. You must pretend commitment and care while you conceal your true aims. It's a lie, of course, but if you lack power it is your only other choice. You must wear two faces, never at the same time, and neither at the wrong time. Fill the workplace with ethical egoists and you create an environment of suspicion, distrust, dishonesty, posturing, and passive aggression.

Even if ethical egoists produce goods and services that benefit others, the world is not a better place because they do. Every self-centered act brings evil into the world. Whatever limited good this philosophy brings about, it plunders the far greater goods of God's glory and the well-being of others, and despoils the joy the Creator intends for our world when we pursue these things.

Hedonism. Another thread in the web of deceit is the belief that self-interest should be about pleasure and pain: maximizing the first and minimizing the second.[7] Hollywood promotes this *ad nauseam*. Madison Avenue assumes that this is the way most people live, and seeks to persuade all to act on these values. Around the clock, every day of the week, countless advertisements through multiple media offer a reduction of pain, the cure of an ill, an increase in libido, weight loss, cosmetic beauty, or the promotion of a vast array of amusements and pleasures. The hucksters are relentless. There is no way to escape them!

When pleasure and pain govern economic activity on a large scale, crass consumerism is the result. Whether something is needed, or is good for society or the environment, is secondary, if not irrelevant. Hedonism's paramount value plays out as a voracious, never-ending consumption in the pursuit of sating ourselves and keeping our mortal pains and discomforts at bay. We become consumer addicts, always on the hunt for our next fix, the next product or service that promises to indulge our desires or palliate our pains. Those who consume become slaves to those who produce.

How does hedonism affect work? Because money secures the ability to maximize pleasure and minimize pain, in a corporate setting everything is reduced to the bottom line of profit. Maximal profit.[8] Those who are at the top enjoy the profits; everyone below them is a means to their ends.[9] It creates a culture of exploitation (for those who have much) and envy (for those who have little). Just compensation, healthy work places, healthy environmental standards, fair business practices, and fair pricing of goods and services have no inherent value or warrant in this vision of life.

If I am a hedonist and I have to choose between my pleasure and your pain? Sorry about your pain! But not really. Better you than me. And if everyone in a company embraces this ethic? Constant calculation: How do I maximize my pleasure and minimize my pain? Constant competition: My pleasure is more important than your pain. Constant conflict: I will pursue my pleasure and protect myself from pain at all costs. Maximal profit is my only interest and minimal sacrifice is my only concern.

Ironically, in a world of hedonists, slaves are not only those who consume, but those who produce. If the bottom line for companies is profit, it inevitably means longer workdays and shorter respites, cancelling family times, giving up vacation days, destroying healthy margins in life, and eliminating wholesome activities and relationships outside of work. All who work become slaves to their work.

Hedonism offers a poor substitute for the lavish joy that God intends for us. (Aquinas observed that the person who is "deprived of spiritual joy goes over to carnal pleasures."[10]) If you have bought into this vision of work, at some point you must ask yourself, "Is this it? Is this all there is? Is it really worthy of my life and my labor? Can I really give myself to this?" You may succeed in increasing your pleasure and decreasing your pain. You will fail utterly in gaining joy. It is a bad deal. You should walk away from it.

Greed and exploitation. These are bound and knotted threads in hell's web of deceit. They are sibling gods before whom we bow to our own demise. Greed motivates acquisition, and exploitation makes greed's ambitions possible. Greed is a ravenous hunger. Exploitation feeds it. Greed is the addiction. Exploitation is the dealer. Greed uses people. It uses and wastes the resources of God's world with little care for the ravaged remains. It cares nothing for future generations, or anyone else in this generation. It is a heartless, soulless, never-resting calculus to enlarge one's hoard.

These vices are not exclusive to any economic class. The grasping, use, and abuse that lie at their heart can be true of the wealthy, the middle class, and the poor.[11] Like a demonic presence, they can possess governments, large corporations, small businesses, and dysfunctional families. They look for any willing host.

We have been led to believe that greed ceases to be a vice when it enters the marketplace. It becomes a good thing. Greed drives capitalism, and capitalism creates wealth for many.[12] To satisfy their avarice, greedy people must provide goods and services for others to purchase. They also need goods and services from others in order to produce the goods and create the services they sell. As everyone pursues their own greed, they provide an unintended good for others. Everyone benefits in the end. So the theory goes.[13]

Greed and joy are dramatically different motivators. They fuel radically different approaches to work.[14] They are fundamentally incompatible. Contradictory. They cannot exist at the same time in the same heart. One will always expel the other. If one wins, the other loses. Greed is grasping; joy is generous. Greed takes; joy gives. Greed hoards; joy shares. Greed domineers; joy serves. Greed seeks gratification; joy seeks the glory of God and the good of others. Greed has no regard for the success of others; joy delights in their accomplishments. Greed cares nothing for quality unless it serves one's self-interest; joy seeks excellence in all things because it honors God, enriches the lives of others, and because there is pleasure in pursuing the best. The good that greed brings about in the marketplace is an unintended outcome (because its only guiding principle is self-interest); the good that joy brings about is purposeful and intentional. Even if greed and joy produce similar goods and services, they create very different worlds.[15]

Careerism. You might agree with what I've written so far but find yourself uneasy and even defensive after reading the first word in this paragraph. "Are you really going to say that a career belongs in the same category as materialism, ethical egoism, hedonism, and greed and exploitation?" Certainly not the work that people do in their careers. If it is honest and wholesome, I applaud it with a whole and merry heart. It is the understanding of work as a career, the pursuit of a career, and the vision of life shaped by our culture's notion of a career that is another thread in the web of lies that ensnare people and keep them from meaningful, joyful work.

In the first half of the last century, a shift took place in our culture's understanding of work. Calling was replaced by career as a way of envisioning work.[16] What people once believed served a larger purpose in God's design for the world became a means of personal gain and fulfillment.[17] Many men were lured into careerism. A spouse at home was just a "house wife." Then the 1960s happened, and what cooked the gander has now cooked the goose. Men and women alike run headlong into a web from which they will not escape with their health, relationships, and faith-commitments intact.

The first problem with careerism for followers of Christ is that it is inherently secular. Atheists can have a career (since it implies nothing about a God), but not a calling (since it implies One who summons us in our work). God is essential to a calling, but optional to a career. At best he is an afterthought, and I can't imagine that this has his approval. If you start your journey on the wrong path, it will not likely end well.[18]

This is not its only problem, however. The notion of a career includes advancement, progress, and moving upward and forward as far as your skills and opportunities will take you. Success is defined by this movement. If advancement in a career is the end you are pursuing, everything else becomes a means. That includes people in your workplace: colleagues, subordinates, and superiors. Their value to you is their ability to help you reach your goals. They are diminished as human beings in their own right. But it doesn't end there. Even if you convince yourself that advancement in your career will benefit your spouse and your children, they, too, will be demeaned. Their rightful place in your life and priorities will be usurped.[19] Your career will be the usurper. Whether it is the loss of shared life, lost opportunities to invest in relationships, lost stability and continuity for your children because you must move again and again to reach your career goals, the losses entailed in careerism are great. Too great.[20] You may climb your way to success, but it will be on the backs of others whom you are called to love.

A career is a cheap substitute for a calling.[21] The problem with careerism is not that it demands too much, though it does; it offers too little. It pretends to be adventurous, but it is not nearly adventurous enough. It mistakes the path of lemmings to a cliff for a great quest in life. God has something that is healthier, more adventurous, more fulfilling, and a better fit for the world that he is seeking to bring about.

Workaholism. When people work too much, it is because something else is wrong. It may be that they have become trapped in the web of deceit that we have been examining. Excessive work may be fueled by a materialistic or hedonistic vision of life, or fed by career ambitions. The problem may be less ambitious: debts to repay or expenses that are greater than one's income. Those who overwork may be single parents with a family whose needs only they can meet. Troubles at home may lie behind long hours at work. Sometimes excessive work masks anxiety: We work too much because we worry that we won't have the financial resources to meet life's demands. Overworking may mask a fear of failure. It may involve an unhealthy sense of duty to an employer or even customers (unhealthy because it supplants loyalty to God, a spouse, and children).

Working too much can be an addiction. We call it *workaholism*. An addiction is a false solution to a true problem: loneliness, depression, low esteem, broken relationships, trauma, emptiness. In a work addiction, addicts find gratification but not fulfillment. They need attention and praise for their long hours and sacrificial work. They need to feel needed, and working excessively meets the need.

Whatever its underlying cause, someone always loses when work becomes an obsession: a husband, a wife, children, family, friends, and workers themselves. Everyone touched by it loses opportunities for joy because work becomes a thief and steals them. If the addiction becomes widespread (as it has), it not only weakens marriages and families, but communities, cities, states, and nations. People may not die from this addiction (though the added stress may bring a premature demise), but it results in work that is not worth doing, and a life that is not worth living.[22]

FALSE GODS

We are not first and foremost *homo faber*.[23] Work is not what is most fundamental about us. We are *homo adorans*.[24] We were made to live every facet of our lives in the worship and enjoyment of God. Everything else is incidental to this. But what happens if we seek to fulfill this Godward dimension with something other than our Creator? Peter Kreeft writes, "Since an idol is not God, no matter how sincerely or passionately it is treated as God, it is bound to break the heart of the worshipper, sooner or later . . . . You can't get blood from a stone or divine joy from nondivine things."[25]

False gods are not only idols; they become demons.[26] When we worship a false god, in time we will be destroyed by it, whether it is money, pleasure, power, or even work. Work is a false god, whether it comes in the guise of Marxism, careerism, or common workaholism. The demonic forces behind it care little which one you choose.

When work ceases to be a false god, it can play its designed role in the worship of God and the service of others. When that happens, the glory is God's, the joy is ours, and a far greater good comes to our world.

QUESTIONS FOR THOUGHT AND DISCUSSION

1. How have you seen practical materialism play out in our culture of work? How does a biblical vision of work correct this? What difference does it make? What difference does it make for you?

2. How have you seen ethical egoism play out in our culture of work? How does a biblical vision of work correct this? What difference does it make?

3. How have you seen hedonism play out in our culture of work? How does a biblical vision of work correct this? What difference does it make?

4. How have you seen careerism play out in our culture of work? How does a biblical vision of work correct this? What difference does it make?

5. How would greed-driven capitalism and joy-inspired capitalism differ from each other? What difference does it make?

CHAPTER 3

JOY AT WORK: REDEMPTION, PART 1

T he Curse will not be fully overcome in this age. Children are born into the world through their mother's painful labor. Work is done by the sweat of our brow. Even if we embrace God's grace in Christ, many do not. Workplaces are often filled with graceless, ungracious people. Even if we reject false views of work, many embrace them. The culture of work is shaped by them. We cannot fully escape the impact.

I wish these things weren't so! The more powerful truth, however, is that what has been transmuted by sin can be transformed by grace. The more work is shaped by Heaven, the better its fit for the earth.[1] The more fully it is formed by Christ and informed by his Word, the more fully it realizes its potential. It becomes good for us, and good for others. It furthers human flourishing. It advances God's glory and increases our joy in life. Because work is such a large part of our existence, redeem work, and the blessings of redemption will change the world.

WORK AND THE NATURAL ORDER

Work is as natural to our lives before God as the cycles of sun and moon:

> He made the moon to mark the seasons;
>> the sun knows its time for setting.
> You make darkness, and it is night,
>> when all the beasts of the forest creep about.
> The young lions roar for their prey,
>> seeking their food from God.
> When the sun rises, they steal away
>> and lie down in their dens.
> Man goes out to his work
>> and to his labor until the evening.
> O LORD, how manifold are your works!
> In wisdom have you made them all;
>> the earth is full of your creatures. (Psalm 104:19-24)

The redemption of work begins when we stop resisting it as something alien to our lives. It begins when we embrace work as part of the natural order of things under God, and when we praise him for his creative wisdom in designing the world this way.

WORK AS GIFT AND PROVISION

The redemption of work continues here. Even if the world often seems inscrutable, there are bedrock truths on which we can base our lives. This is the message of Ecclesiastes:

> What gain has the worker from his toil? I have seen the business that God has given to the children of man to be busy with. He has made everything beautiful in its time. Also, he has put eternity into man's heart, yet so that he cannot find out what God has done from the beginning to the end. I perceived that there is nothing better for them than to be joyful and to do good as long as they live; also that everyone should eat and drink and take pleasure in all his toil—this is God's gift to man. (Ecclesiastes 3:9-13)

Joy in our work and pleasure in our toil is a gift from God. It is essential to flourishing in life. The redemption of work takes place as we embrace what God has given to enrich and enhance our lives.

When we pray, "Give us this day our daily bread,"[2] God could answer by providing for us as he did the ancient people of Israel with manna and quail in the wilderness.[3] But his response normally involves human labor: from ranches and farms to markets, from markets to kitchens, from kitchens to tables. Whether we are personally involved in this process, God's provision includes our labor, which makes it possible for us to benefit from the work of farmers, ranchers, truckers, and grocers. Work is an answer to our prayer for provision, which makes it something for which we should be thankful. As often as we eat, we should thank God for the meal before us and for the loving hands behind it: the hands that were given to its preparation, and the many others that were involved in making it possible.

WORKING FOR GOD

Adam worked for God. Animals received thoughtful names and a Garden was cultivated because this was so.[4] We are called to work for God, too. This vision of labor has been lost in our day. (Sadly, this is often true even for those who see themselves living in the realm of grace. It is a disgrace. We would lose our jobs if we ignored our employers the way we disregard the Lord of our work!) It is not only a shame, but folly. The loss of this perspective, which has resulted in the secularization of work, lies behind many of the woes in the workplace today.

The apostle Paul saw human labor as work for God. The economic system in his day revolved around masters and slaves, but the underlying truths hold for all who work:

> Bondservants, obey your earthly masters with fear and trembling, with a sincere heart, as you would Christ, doing the will of God from the heart, rendering service with a good will as to the Lord and not to man. . . . Masters, do the same to them, and stop your threatening, knowing that he who is both their Master and yours in heaven, and that there is no partiality with him. (Ephesians 6:5-9)

> Bondservants, obey in everything those who are your earthly masters, no by way of eye-service, as people-pleasers, but with sincerity of heart, fearing the Lord. Masters, treat your bondservants justly and fairly, knowing that you also have a Master in heaven. (Colossians 3:21-4:1) [5]

Work done for God inspires good will. When it is done as service to Christ, it brings honesty to every endeavor. There is no need for intimidation, because all do their work heartily. Those who have authority treat others justly and fairly because they see themselves under a higher Authority. All do their work before the Lord of all work – the One for whom there is no menial task and no regard for rank. No amount of government regulations can bring these things about. Change work in these ways and the world will be a very different place!

WORK AS STEWARDSHIP

In one of his parables, Jesus told the story of a man who left his estate to travel to another place. In his stead, he appointed servants to continue his enterprises, and gave them funds in different amounts with which to work. When he returned after a long absence, he called his servants to give an accounting of what they had done with the resources he had entrusted to them. Two of them doubled the funds which they had been given; one did nothing to increase his master's capital. Only the first two received his commendation: "Well done, good and faithful servant. You have been faithful over a little; I will set you over much. Enter into the joy of your master.'"[6]

We may not have many choices in the work we do. We may not control its profitability. But we are all called to steward the work God has assigned to us. He enlists us to manage resources, responsibilities, and opportunities for him. Wherever you find workers who see themselves as stewards under God, you will also find industry, diligence, a commitment to excellence, fairness in pricing and practices, and a commitment to the good of fellow workers and customers alike. Whether they make little or much, if they steward well the opportunities and responsibilities God gives them in their work, the best part of their work is the joy that he gives.

WORK AS WORSHIP

It was the Greeks, not the Jews, who belittled work.[7] For the former, most work was fit only for slaves.[8] Slave labor freed the landed elite to pursue a life of leisure. In a Jewish vision of life, work connects us with God (as all of life can). It is from him, enabled by him, and in worship, offered back to him. Work may be demanding, but it is not demeaning. Even if it is humble in the eyes of some, it is honored in the eyes of our God. If it is acknowledged as a gift and a charge from God, received with a willing and thankful heart, and offered to God for his greater glory in the world, work is as much an act of worship as anything we do.[9]

Work as liturgy. When work fulfills God's intentions it becomes a liturgy in life. You may know how this word is used in church settings (the customs of public worship), but you may not know that it comes from the Greek word *leitourgos*, (*leitos*, meaning public and *ergos*, meaning work). In ancient Greece, *leitourgos* referred to work undertaken for the community.[10]

It was work done for the common good. It took on fresh nuances in the New Testament. Note the words in italics:

> And every priest stands daily at his *service*, offering repeatedly the same sacrifices. (Hebrews 10:11)

> And there was a prophetess, Anna . . . . She did not depart from the temple, *worshiping* with fasting and prayer night and day (Luke 2:37)

> Because of the grace of God given me by God to be a *minister* of Christ Jesus to the Gentiles . . . . (Romans 15:16)

> "For because of this you also pay taxes, for the authorities are *ministers* of God, attending to this very thing." (Romans 13:6)

What do the duties of a priest, the worship of a prophetess, the mission of an apostle, and the work of civic ruler have in common? They are united in this word, *leitourgos*.[11] All can be acts of worship. In a Christian vision of life, when work is directed to God and serves the good of others, it is worship, whether you are a pastor or a postal worker, a merchant or a missionary.[12]

Work as an oblation. An oblation is something offered to God in worship. Ancient Jewish people offered animals or grain. Where did these offerings come from? From flocks, herds, and crops. But where did they come from? From the Creator, true. All of creation is his.[13] But there is more to an oblation than this. Sheep and cattle must be raised, and crops must be planted, cultivated, and harvested if they are to be offered to God.[14] Oblations involve our work.

All that is from God is to be offered back to him. In the process it passes through human hands. For ancient believers, animals and grain offered to God in worship represented the work of farmers and shepherds, or the work of merchants, artisans, or craftsmen whose labor allowed them to purchase these things for their offerings to God. It was not only that offerings were made possible by work, they signified one's work, offered to God. Work and worship were woven into a single cloth. The same is true for us. The offering of our financial resources in worship represents our work. If we understand what we are doing, our offering is not money, but money as a token of our work. Our livelihood. Our daily tasks. It is an oblation that is pleasing to our God.[15]

Much more than we thought. Too many Christians in our day privatize worship. It is what we do in "quiet times," or when we join others in listening to sermons, and singing songs of worship and praise. This is a stunted view of worship. Life as a whole, including our work, is meant to be an expression of worship. If we pursue life the way God means us to, the study of his Word, private prayer and corporate worship will be integral to a larger pattern of worshiping God by seeking his glory and enjoying him in everything that fills our days.

Nearly a century ago, Dutch statesman, philosopher, theologian, and educator, Abraham Kuyper, wrote: "There is not a square inch in the whole domain of our human existence, over which Christ, who is sovereign over all, does not cry "Mine!""[16] C.S. Lewis put it this way:

> It is not so much of our time and so much of our attention that God demands; it is not even all our time and all our attention; it is ourselves. . . . What cannot be admitted – what must exist only as an undefeated but daily resisted enemy – is the idea of something that is "our own," some area in which we are to be "out of school," on which God has no claim.[17]

Those who worship truly embrace this as a way of life.

WORK AS A GOOD WORK

Best-selling author, Robert Bellah, comments on the increasing focus on the individual in American culture, and sees our generation trapped in an irony:

> But there is another problem, a very big problem, and its solution is hard to envision. Just when we are moving to an ever greater validation of the sacredness of the individual person, our capacity to imagine a social fabric that would hold individuals together is vanishing. This is in part because of the fact that the religious individualism that I have been describing is linked to an economic individualism which, ironically, knows nothing of the sacredness of the individual. Its only standard is money, and the only thing more sacred than money is more money.[18]

The proposal he and his colleagues make to transform the American business culture?

> To make a real difference . . . a shift in rewards would have to be a part of reappropriation of the idea of vocation or calling, a return in a new way to the idea of work as a contribution to the good of all and not merely as a means to one's own advancement.[19]

Christians have something significant to offer the world. Our offering lies in what Jesus and his early disciples called *good works*. We are called to do them as we follow him.

Let me define a good work as any task that is done for the glory of God and the good of another.[20] It fulfills the greatest commands to love God supremely and our neighbors as ourselves. A good work is undertaken from our love for God and our commitment to his glory in the world. It seeks to honor him in the eyes of others. It embraces the words of Jesus: "Let your light shine before others, so that they may see your good works and give glory to your Father who is in heaven."[21] Good works benefit others. They meet needs, enrich, and bless. They make it possible for others to flourish in life. They are expressions of love, undertaken with joy. Luther was right:

> Love does not think about doing works, it finds joy in people; and when something good is done for others, that does not appear to love as works but simply as gifts which flow naturally from love.[22]

> It is his neighbor in whom the new man finds his joy. That which takes place between him and his neighbor is not works, the righteousness of which is of concern to him; he does not ask about the worth of what he does. He sees only a neighbor who awakens gladness in him.[23]

> Our neighbor with his need does not press upon us against our will; rather he fills us with gladness, for it is our joy to serve him.[24]

Good works are a way of living lovingly and joyfully in the world.[25] If joy is the beatitude of love for God and others, and good works are an expression of that love, joy is inevitable – like standing beneath a fountain and getting wet, or standing next to a fire and getting warm.[26] First century Christians knew this well:

> We want you to know, brothers, about the grace of God that has been given among the churches of Macedonia, for in a severe test of affliction, their abundance of joy and their extreme poverty have overflowed in a wealth of generosity on their part. For they gave according to their means, as I can testify, and beyond their means, of their own accord, begging us earnestly for the favor of taking part in the relief of the saints. (2 Corinthians 8:1-4)

Where there is joy, there is no sense of duty or sacrifice, only a cheerful heart that pursues the well-being of others.

We tend to think of good works as actions we undertake in the role of a volunteer: Saturday morning at a homeless shelter, or mentoring a troubled teen. I don't wish to disparage this; however, if you accept the claims I've made about work in a joyful vision of life, you will see that work itself can be a good work. If we do it for the glory of God and the good of others, it is. If we do it heartily for the Lord, and it is a joy for us to see others benefit from our labor, it is.

Not only can work be a good work, the financial resources generated by our work can provide opportunities for good works. Read these apostolic words with care: "Let the thief no longer steal, but rather let him labor, doing honest work with his own hands, so that he may have something to share with anyone in need."[27] What kind of work should we do? Honest work. Why should we work? The implicit reason is to provide for ourselves rather than taking from others; the explicit reason is to share with others in need.

We should work for the glory of God and the good of others. If we do this well and profit from it, it will be a joy to share with others, whether it is a company profit-sharing plan or personal generosity to the poor. There are no guarantees that joyful work will generate profit, but it often will, and when it does, it is a good work if it shares its boon:

> As for the rich in this present age, charge them not to be haughty, nor to set their hopes on the uncertainty of riches, but on God, who richly provides us with everything to enjoy. They are to do good, to be rich in good works, to be generous and ready to share, thus storing up treasure for themselves as a good foundation for the future, so that they may take hold of that which is truly life. (1 Timothy 6:17-19)

If we pursue work this way, it will transform our daily tasks. Karl Barth wrote of those who learn this joy, "[They] will not only seek joy somewhere apart as the joy of Sundays or holidays but also in the midst of their everyday work. And perhaps it is to be found here in its purest and strongest terms."[28] If we discover this joy, we will touch and enrich the lives of others. More than that, we may well bring about a humble but powerful revolution in the workplaces of the world.

QUESTIONS FOR THOUGHT AND DISCUSSION

1. What difference does it make to view your work as working for God?

2. Discuss this quote in the context of your own work and workplace: "If you find workers who see themselves as stewards under God, you will also find industry, diligence, a commitment to excellence, fairness in pricing and practices, and a commitment to the good of fellow workers and customers alike."

3. What difference will it make in the following week if you view your work as an act of worship? Are there obstacles you will have to overcome to do this? If so, what are they?

4. Would you say that you have tended to privatize and compartmentalize worship? What difference will it make for you to break down walls between "sacred" and "secular" in your life?

5. If a good work is "any task that is done for the glory of God and the good of others," how can your work become a good work?

CHAPTER 4

JOY AT WORK: REDEMPTION, PART 2

N orman Wirzba writes, "Our entire life, and thus also our work, must be understood and carried out in orientation and conversation with God."[1]   If you do this, you will find your work wonderfully transformed. But there is even better news than this. What if I told you that the Maker of the Universe and the Lord of All Ages is so committed to your work that he wants to join you in it? That he offers his help? That his empowering presence can energize you for your tasks? People who know much more about God and his ways than I do have said that this is so:

> [Nehemiah on the rebuilding of the wall in Jerusalem] "But now, O God, strengthen my hands." (Nehemiah 6:9)

> [Upon the completion of the work] They perceived that this work had been accomplished with the help of our God. (Nehemiah 6:16)

> May the favor of the LORD our God rest upon us; establish the work of our hands for us – yes, establish the work of our hands. (Psalm 90:17, NIV)

Unless the LORD builds the house, those who build it labor in vain. (Psalm 127:1)

For this I toil, struggling with all his energy that he powerfully works within me. (Colossians 1:29)

Now to him who is able to do far more abundantly than all that we ask or think, according to the power at work within us, to him be glory in the church and in Christ Jesus throughout all generations, forever and ever. Amen. (Ephesians 2:20-21)

Finally, be strong in the Lord and in the strength of his might. (Ephesians 6:10)

If we see the world truly, and our work clearly, we will rise each morning thankful for the work God has given us, with a sense of wonder that God himself will strengthen our hands. We will venture eagerly into the day knowing that God will join us in our labor, and that he will work through our work to accomplish his purposes in the world.

The word *synergism* helps us understand a Christian vision of work. It comes from the Greek, combining a noun, *ergos*, or work, and a preposition, *syn*, which means together.[2] Synergism is about working together. Here we discover something very important about God's design for work. He intends it to be collaborative. Cooperative. First, we work with God; he works with us. We participate in his work; he shares in ours. The apostle Paul wrote, "For we are God's fellow workers" (*synergoi*).[3] In these words we see not only the work of redemption (the labor of an apostle) but the redemption of work. Imagine working shoulder to shoulder with God, moving in the same direction toward the same goal! When our work aligns with God's purposes, he does not stand to the side and watch. He joins us. We become fellow workers with God. (If this prospect isn't stunning to you, you are still a stranger to its significance. Stop here. Ponder and then wonder!)

Synergism also describes the rhythm of people working together. At its best, work is teamwork. It is a community project. Paul also wrote, "We work with you (*synergeo*) for your joy."[4] If we read them without dividing life into artificial categories of sacred and secular, these words have great power. Our salvation is in view, but redemption is meant to include everything in our lives, including our work. Imagine workplaces with this motto: Working with you for your joy! The joy of collaboration is a connection with God (as all joy is) as we join him in his work, he joins us in ours, and we share joy with all who join us in the task. When we pray for God's Kingdom to come and his will to be done on earth as it is in heaven, this is one way in which God answers our prayer.[5]

WORK AND VOCATION

In contemporary vernacular, vocational schools are for those who don't pursue a college degree. Earn a diploma from a vocational school and become a worker bee; earn a degree from a university and become a beekeeper. This is not the first time that vocation has been used to drive a wedge between people whom God would have flourish in life together. In medieval Europe only clergy had a vocation, or calling from God. Everyone else just worked. It fit the ecclesiastical division of life between sacred and secular, and the supremacy of the sacred (i.e., the domain of the church). Martin Luther challenged this with the revolutionary idea, grounded in the Scriptures, that all believers are priests.[6] Because this is so, all have a vocation, or calling from God, whether they wear a clerical robe or a smithy apron, whether they baptize babies or change their diapers.[7]

Luther wrote:

> What you do in your house is worth as much as if you did it up in
> heaven for our Lord God. For what we do in our calling here on
> earth in accordance with His word and command He counts as if it
> were done in Heaven for Him . . . .

> Therefore we should accustom ourselves to think of our position
> and work as sacred and well-pleasing to God, not on account of the
> position and the work, but on account of the word and faith from
> which the obedience and the work flow. No Christian should
> despise his position and life if he is living in accordance with the
> word of God, but should say, "I believe in Jesus Christ, and do as
> the ten commandments teach, and pray that our dear Lord God
> may help me thus to do." That is a right and holy life, and cannot
> be made holier even if one fast himself to death.[8]

Elsewhere he wrote, "Every occupation has its own honor before God."[9]
And, "What seem to be secular works are actually the praise of God and
represent an obedience which is well–pleasing to him."[10]

To parents whose children take roles in human government, Luther
wrote:

> It ought to be a matter of great honor and satisfaction for you to
> see your son an angel in the empire and an apostle of the emperor,
> a cornerstone and bulwark of temporal peace on earth, knowing for
> a certainty that God so regards it and it really is true. For although
> such works do not make men righteous before God or save them,
> nevertheless, it is a joy and comfort to know these works please
> God so very much – and the more so when such a man is a believer
> and is in the kingdom of Christ, for he thereby thanks God for his
> benefits, bringing to him the finest thankoffering, the highest
> service.[11]

For those who became doctors, he wrote, "It is not the practice of medicine alone, however, but Scripture too that shows it to be a useful, comforting, and salutary estate, as well as a service acceptable to God, made and founded by him."[12]

Calvin later added:

> The Lord enjoins every one of us, in all the actions of life, to have respect to our own calling. He . . . has assigned distinct duties to each in the different modes of life. And that no one may presume to overstep his proper limits, he has distinguished the different modes of life by the name of callings. Every man's mode of life, therefore, is a kind of station assigned him by the Lord. . . in following your proper calling, no work will be so mean and sordid as not to have a splendour and value in the eye of God.[13]

The loss of meaningful (and joyful) work in our world is directly related to the loss of these perspectives.[14] With no guiding belief that God has commissioned the human race to make something of the world he created, with no vision of living for the glory of God and the good of others, and with no sense that our tasks are a calling from God, the resulting secularization reduces work to payroll activity.

God calls us; work is our response. He commissions us; we steward the charge. But there is more to it than this. Vocation is not first what we do for God; it is God's way of accomplishing his purposes through us. We can't begin to count the things God does without our participation. Stars blaze and burn out, and we only learn about it (if we ever do) light-years after the fact. The earth spins on its axis and flies around the sun without our hands. Autumn leaves fall to the ground without even a thought from us. But in the world of history, and the creating and shaping of cultures and civilizations, God has chosen to work through human agents.

God works through our work. Ours may be the hands that others see, but the unseen hand of God upholds ours and works through them. Paul could speak of his "work for God," and then refer to it as what "Christ has accomplished through me."[15] You might be tempted to say, "But his was the work of an apostle. It was spiritual work." Don't go there! It is a false path. Paul viewed his work, and God's work through him, as part of a larger pattern: "From him and through him and to him are all things."[16] That includes your work and mine. This is closer to the truth:

> God is milking the cows through the vocation of the milkmaid, said Luther. According to Luther, vocation is a "mask of God." He is hidden in vocation. We see the milkmaid, or the farmer, or the doctor or pastor or artist. But, looming behind this human mask, God is genuinely present and active in what they do for us.[17]

VOCATION AND EMPLOYMENT

"What if my vocation and my employment don't match? What if job opportunities aren't available for me in the area I believe my calling to be? I'm not in a position to wait for employment that fits my vocation: I have bills to pay! I have a family to provide for!"

Good questions. My first response is that it is a popular but mistaken belief that our vocation must be remunerated. You may or may not receive financial compensation for your special calling. The apostle Paul did not.[18] It may or may not coincide with your employment. In fact it may be what some call an *avocation*! Maybe your calling is to steward your sensitive soul and compelling desire to help others in need, and you fulfill this in the course of a week as you interact with people and volunteer at a homeless shelter on Saturday mornings. Maybe your special calling is to steward your artistic gifts for the glory of God and the good of others, and you fulfill that in the decoration of your home, the presentation of meals at your table, and displaying your artwork at a local nursing home to enrich the lives of forgotten people. Maybe God is calling you to steward your athletic abilities and experience, and you fulfill that by being a volunteer coach at your local recreation center.[19] It is a wonderful concurrence when our livelihood and our vocation match, but vocation is bigger than this.

My second response to these questions is that they are based on too narrow a view of vocation. We don't have just one vocation. We have several. In a robust Christian vision of life, work is always related to vocation. Always. Let me give you a diagram of our callings in life.

CIRCLES OF CALLING

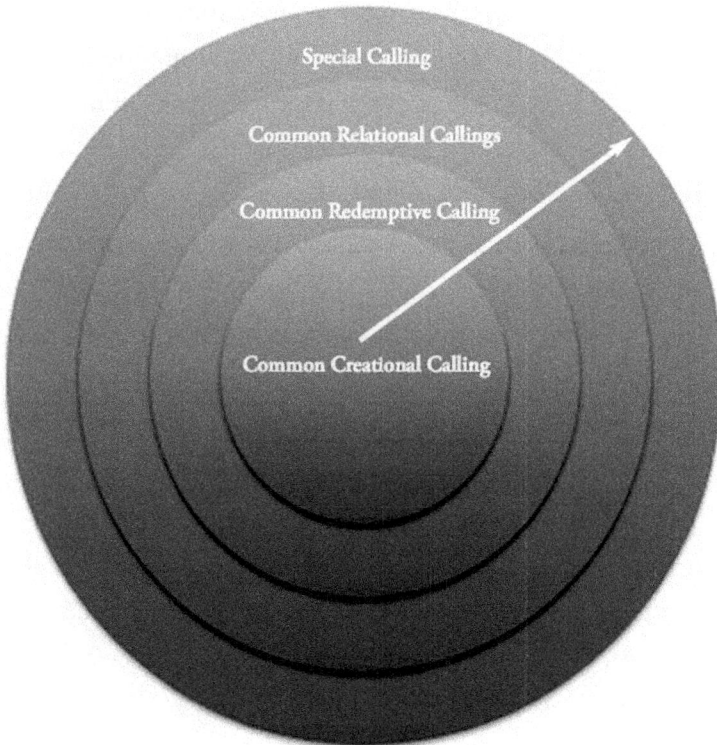

Special Calling

Common Relational Callings

Common Redemptive Calling

Common Creational Calling

The innermost circle in the diagram above represents our common creational calling. By virtue of being human we are called to glorify God and enjoy him forever.[20] As image-bearers of God, we are called to be his vice-regents in the world, stewarding resources and developing potential to create a healthy habitat for humanity. Whatever your employment may be, this is your first vocation.

The next circle outward represents our common redemptive calling. If you have embraced Christ, you have a common calling with all who have done the same. God calls us into "the fellowship of his Son, Jesus Christ our Lord."[21] We are called to live in the Kingdom of God and to live as its representatives and agents in the world.[22] Whatever we do in word or deed, we are called to do it "in the name of the Lord Jesus, giving thanks to God the Father through him."[23] It is not true that some Christians have this calling, and others don't. It is common to all who name the name of Christ. Whatever your daily work may be, this is your second vocation.

As we move outward, the next circle represents common relational callings. It is God who calls men to be husbands and fathers. If you have this calling, you share its essential responsibilities with all who are Christian husbands and fathers. It is God who calls women to be wives and mothers. If you have this calling, you share its essential responsibilities with all women who are Christian wives and mothers. If you are a parent, you share a calling with all parents. If you are a child, you share a calling with all children. Whatever your work may be, you have very important callings here.

The outermost circle in the diagram represents your special calling. This is specific to you. No one else can fulfill this vocation. It has your name on it. It is yours alone. Just as Paul was called to be an apostle,[24] God has a calling for you to fulfill in the world. This is what many people have in mind when they think about their vocation.

Let's say you believe that your special calling is to steward your abilities as an engineer for the glory of God and the good of others. If you are paid to do this, wonderful! But what if you are unable to find employment as an engineer? Let's also say that you are married and have children. The employment you are able to find may not connect with your special calling, but it does fulfill an important part of God's calling in your life as a husband and father, or as a wife and mother. If you are a provider for your parents in their elder years, your work is an important part of God's calling in your life as a child. (We don't stop being children in God's eyes just because we reach a certain age or achieve financial independence. We simply become adult children.)

Whether you are married or not, have children or not, have living parents or not, if your employment does not fulfill your special calling, it nevertheless can and should fulfill your creational calling and your calling as a follower of Christ. Whatever your special calling may be, you should affirm and embrace these truths about your work:

> ➢ Joy in your work and pleasure in your toil is a gift from God

> ➢ Work is an answer to your prayers for provision.

> ➢ God himself will give you strength and ability to do your work.

> ➢ You can glorify God and enjoy him through your work.

> ➢ Whatever your task, you work for God.

➤ Your work can fulfill God's intentions for you as an image-bearer in his world.

➤ Whether they are great or small, God has put you where you are to steward opportunities and responsibilities.

➤ Your work can be an act of worship, signaling the consecration of your life to God.

➤ Your work can be a good work, an expression of your love for God and your love for others.

No follower of Jesus just has a job. If you think otherwise, you've been misled. You are mistaken. Won't you agree with God about your work and your callings in life? He wants far more for you than you have imagined!

DISCOVERING YOUR SPECIAL CALLING

In my work with university students over the years I've often been asked, "How can I discover God's calling for my life? How can I learn what he intends my unique contribution to his Kingdom to be?" If you are asking this for yourself, I will give you the best counsel I have.

Seek first the Kingdom. No matter what your need or uncertainty may be, you will only discover God's provision if seeking his Kingdom is first in your priorities.[25] Kingdom-seeking aligns your heart with God's. It frames life so that you will be able to see things in a God-centered way. I say much more about this in other works,[26] but here let me pass along words of wisdom from Dallas Willard:

So when Jesus directs us to pray, "Thy Kingdom come," he does not mean we should pray for it to come into existence. Rather, we pray it to take over all points in the personal, social, and political order where it is now excluded: "On earth as it is in heaven." With this prayer we are invoking it, as in faith we are acting it, into the real world of our daily existence.[27]

This is where the search for your special calling must begin.

Follow Christ wherever he leads. Don't even entertain the thought, "I'm staying put until I discover God's calling for my life." Follow Christ wherever he leads you, and do this every day. Even if you don't know your special calling, follow Christ as a way of life and you will be in the best position to hear God's calling when it comes. If you don't do this, I can't offer hope that you will ever hear from God.

Focus first on your common callings. Your question concerns the special calling God has for you. But if you are a follower of Christ, you already have callings to which you must attend. Os Guinness wrote: "Calling is the truth that God calls us to himself so decisively that everything we are, everything we do, and everything we have is invested with a special devotion, dynamism, and direction lived out as a response to his summons and service."[28]

Whatever you do, your work can fulfill your part in the creation mandate, stewarding the resources of the earth, and maximizing the gifts and talents God has given you for his glory and the good of others. This is no small thing! With all who follow Christ, you have been called into fellowship with him.[29] You've been called into the Kingdom of God.[30] You've been called to holy living.[31] You have been called to honor Christ in your work.[32] If you are a Christian husband and father, you share a calling with all Christian men who are husbands and fathers. If you are a Christian wife and mother, you share a calling with all Christian women who are wives and mothers. If your parents are living, you share a calling with all children to honor your father and mother. If you are a student, you share a calling common to all students to love God with your mind, and to steward this time in your life for the glory of God. Fulfill these callings well!

Act on what you already know to be true. There is an important spiritual principle that to receive more from God, we must first act on what we have already been given.[33] To learn more we must first implement what we already know to be true. You might lack vocational guidance, but you already have moral guidance in the Scriptures. If you fail to act on the moral guidance God has already given you, you will never recognize his vocational guidance when it comes. Love God wholly and supremely, and love your neighbor as yourself.[34] Habituate your heart in these loves and you will be in the best position to hear from God. If you pursue joy in all the ways I've written about in *Path of Life* and *River of Delights*, your life will be fruitful and fulfilling even if you don't yet know the unique vocation God has for you. If you are flourishing in a joyful life before God you will be in the best place to hear his voice when he speaks.

Understand who you are as God's workmanship. The apostle Paul wrote: "For we are his workmanship, created in Christ Jesus for good works, which he prepared beforehand for us to walk in."[35] The good works God has for you to do are related to who you are as his workmanship. If you think that you are called to be a professional athlete, but you haven't been equipped with stellar physical skills, you will waste your time waiting for a contract. If you believe that your calling is to be a chef, but no one will eat what you put on the table, you should probably explore your calling elsewhere. Your sense of calling may only be masked envy of someone else who has that calling. It can happen. It often does. Understanding who you are as the handiwork of God is a good place to start as you think about his calling in your life.

Frederick Buechner wrote, "The place God calls you to is the place where your deep gladness and the world's deep hunger meet."[36] What do you enjoy doing? What are you passionate about? What brings you great joy when you do it? What grips your heart with concern? What breaks your heart and compels you to do something? What tasks energize you? What do others invite you to do? Where do others ask for your help? In what ways do they seek your involvement in their lives? Questions like these, pondered prayerfully, will point you in fruitful directions.

Steward your talents, opportunities, and responsibilities. God has already given you responsibilities. He has given you talents. He will give you opportunities. It is likely that you already know some of them. The foolish person says, "I'm staying where I am until God reveals his calling to me." God is never held hostage to our terms. He probably laughs at them. The wise person says, "I will give myself fully and joyfully to my responsibilities and to the opportunities that come to me. I will seek to honor my Lord by giving him my best, and trust that in 'an acceptable time' I will learn his special calling for me."[37] Do this, and prepare to hear from God.

Seek godlywise counsel. By the time you finish reading this book, I hope you will be persuaded that God's design for your life is fulfilled in community. It is the way he has made us. It is the way he relates to us. It is the way he brings about Christ-likeness in us. It is the way most of his guidance will be given to us. Listen to the people who know you well, who have observed your life, and who are committed to you. Listen to people who know God's Word, and whose lives have been shaped by it. Listen to the people who are walking a path that leads them into a greater knowledge of God and his ways. Ask them to pray for you about your vocation. Ask them to pray with you. And then be alert to what God brings from this.

Ask God, then listen. It is God's part to call; it is ours to listen for his summons. We should ask him to show us his calling for our lives, and then pay attention. Jesus said:

Ask, and it will be given to you; seek and you will find; knock, and it will be opened to you. For everyone who asks receives, and the one who seeks finds, and to the one who knocks it will be opened. Or which one of you, if his son asks him for bread, will give him a stone? Or if he asks for a fish, will give him a serpent? If you then, who are evil, know how to give good gifts to your children, how much more will your Father who is in heaven give good things to those who ask him! (Matthew 7:7-11)

One who knew Jesus well wrote, "If any of you lacks wisdom, let him ask God, who gives generously to all without reproach, and it will be given him."[38] It is not God's intent to hide our calling from us. How could it be? But I can believe that he might wait to disclose it to us until he knows the time is right. God is generous, but never wasteful with his guidance and direction. He never speaks to hear himself. He does not speak to have his word fall on deaf ears. He waits until he sees this posture of heart:

Speak, LORD, for your servant is listening. (Samuel, 1 Samuel 3:10)

What am I to do, Lord? (Saul of Tarsus, Acts 22:10)

Here am I, LORD, send me! (Isaiah, Isaiah 6:8)

Take intentional steps of faith in the direction of your prayers. The verses that follow God's promise to give us wisdom go on to say: "But let him ask in faith, with no doubting, for the one who doubts is like a wave of the sea that is driven and tossed by the wind. For that person must not suppose that he will receive anything from the Lord; he is a double-minded man, unstable in all his ways."[39] God waits for faith-filled hearts. He looks for hearts that believe him, embrace his promises, and are ready act on his Word.

This is the way Jesus described this faith:

> Have faith in God. Truly, I say to you, whoever says to this
> mountain, "Be taken up and thrown into the sea," and does not
> doubt in his heart, but believes that what he says will come to pass,
> it will be done for him. Therefore I tell you, whatever you ask in
> prayer, believe that you have received it, and it will be yours. (Mark
> 11:23-24)

I confess that my prayers are more often, "I believe. Help my unbelief!"[40] If
the faith that moves mountains is the size of a mustard seed,[41] mine is
microscopic. What hope is there for me? My personal resolve in life is to
pray, and then take intentional steps of faith in the direction of my prayers.
They may be small steps, even very small steps, but each one takes me farther
from where I am, and that much closer to the objective of my prayer. Even if
God desires greater faith, he accepts the little faith that we act on. God
discloses his calling when he knows that the one who receives his call will
respond in obedient faith.

If you wait to act until everything is clear to you, you may wait the rest of
your life. Don't let "Died waiting" be the epitaph on your gravestone! Act on
the little God shows you, and he will show you more. Maybe you have a gift
and passion for teaching. Maybe you are drawn to people in need and are
strongly motivated to help them. Maybe you can organize people and you
enjoy accomplishing tasks and reaching goals. Maybe you feel fully alive
when you get to problem-solve for people who are confused and frustrated in
life. Whatever it may be, seek direction from God, and then look for
opportunities to fulfill the desires and use the gifts he has given you. Offer
your talents and passions to God, and start looking for opportunities. Make
it a daily practice to take intentional steps of faith in the direction of your
prayers.

Shhh. I think I hear a Voice calling!

QUESTIONS FOR THOUGHT AND DISCUSSION

1. Discuss the following quote in the context of your day-to-day work:

   > What if I told you that the Maker of the Universe and the Lord of All Ages is so committed to your work that he wants to join you in it? That he offers his help? That his empowering presence can energize you for your tasks? People who know much more about God and his ways than I do have said that this is so.

2. How does work-as-vocation differ from work-as-a-career, and how will you let this illumine your understanding of your work?

3. Discuss the following quote about Luther's understanding of vocation:

   > God is milking the cows through the vocation of the milkmaid, said Luther. According to Luther, vocation is a "mask of God." He is hidden in vocation. We see the milkmaid, or the farmer, or the doctor or pastor or artist. But, looming behind this human mask, God is genuinely present and active in what they do for us.

4. Review the chapter's diagram and discussion of vocations in our lives, and then talk about what difference it makes when you view your daily tasks in this light.

5. If you don't know your "special calling," how does this chapter's discussion give you guidance in pursuing this?

CHAPTER 5

JOY AT REST
SABBATH, PART 1

M any of us yearn for rest because we've burned out from too much work. Life is frenetic. Harried. Exhausting. We know it isn't healthy, but we feel trapped. We can't get off the spinning treadmill. Rest beckons. It's what we desperately want and need, but can't find in the madness of the marketplace. Every time we move toward it with hopeful hearts we are dragged back, captive to forces we no longer control. The only sound we hear is the din of demands. The clamor of competition. If we don't move with the masses, somehow stay ahead of them, we will be trampled. So we keep working, working, working. There must be a better way. There is! It is the ancient practice of Sabbath.

THE SABBATH CUP: CELEBRATING CREATION

Imagine a cup and a pitcher held above it, pouring clear, cool water for thirsty wayfarers. You are one of them. Unless you drink, you cannot take another step. The water poured into this cup is the meaning of the Sabbath and its significance for your life. Here is the first decanting of liquid refreshment: The Sabbath is God's invitation to share his joy in creation.

> Thus the heavens and the earth were finished, and all the host of them. And on the seventh day God finished his work that he had done, and he rested on the seventh day from all his work that he had done. So God blessed the seventh day and made it holy, because on it God rested from all his work that he had done in creation. (Genesis 2:1-3)

Why did God rest? To catch his breath after creating a universe billions of light years from one end to the other? No, nothing diminishes an Almighty God. He never grows weary or tired.[1] The inspired Story of Beginnings gives us a different clue: When God finished his work of creation, he pronounced it "very good."[2] It is as if he stepped back to take pleasure in his work, to appreciate and enjoy the cosmos that leapt into being at his command. The Creator ceased in order to savor. He rested in order to rejoice in what he had done. This is the first meaning of the Sabbath.

This is the first meaning of the Sabbath for us, as well. The Sabbath creates time and space in our schedules for enjoying God and his handiwork in our world. We see this in an ancient Psalm written for the Sabbath:

> For you, O LORD, have made me glad by your work;
>   At the works of your hands I sing for joy.
> How great are your works, O LORD!
>   Your thoughts are very deep! (Psalm 92:4-5)[3]

Joyful rest is the centerpiece of the Sabbath. It is not a tedious inconvenience that we must endure before we can get on with what we really want to do. God invites us to experience the Sabbath as a delight.[4] There is rest for our bodies and refreshment for our souls when we devote time in our week to the enjoyment of God and the world he has made, and we share these joys together.[5] God designed our Sabbath to be a participation in his own sabbatical pleasure.[6]

THE SABBATH CUP: SACRED PATTERNS

Spring, summer, fall, winter. New moon, crescent moons, full moon. Evening, morning, afternoon. There are cadences in creation. Patterns in the fabric of the world. This is how we are introduced to the Sabbath. It is a salient feature in the sacred configuration of life:

> Remember the Sabbath day, to keep it holy. Six days you shall labor, and do all your work; but the seventh day is a Sabbath to the LORD God; in it you shall not do any work, you, or your son, or your daughter, your manservant, or your maidservant, or your cattle, or the sojourner who is within your gates; for in six days the LORD made heaven and earth, the sea, and all that is in them, and rested the seventh day; therefore the Lord blessed the Sabbath day and hallowed it. (Exodus 20:8-11)[7]

This is the second decanting of significance into the Sabbath cup: The Sabbath is God's invitation to join him in a sacred pattern of life.[8]

The Sabbath puts a limit on work in our lives. Work is something, but not everything. It is important, but not ultimate. God is, which brings us to a second truth about this day: It is not simply a Sabbath, but a "Sabbath to the Lord." He is the focus of this day. What we do, we do *coram Deo*, before the face of God, in his presence, under his lordship, consecrated to his purposes, for his glory in the world.

The Sabbath commemorates God's work of creation, and the rhythm of work and rest in his design. Without rest our heart's attention would too easily be riveted on the acquisition of goods and services to sustain our physical life. Too easily, the Creator would be eclipsed in our thoughts by the never-ending challenges of our creature-life. We need this time to cultivate a centered focus on our Maker. It allows us to align our hearts with God and to harmonize our wills with his.

The Sabbath has been blessed by the Lord. This is what Jesus had in mind, I think, when he said that the Sabbath was "made for man."[9] It was designed for our good. It contributes to a robust life. Part of the blessing is respite from work to renew our bodies and refresh our souls. Habituating our lives in this healthy pattern also allows us to break the power of stress during our work week. The Psalmist wrote: "It is in vain that you rise up early and go late to rest, eating the bread of anxious toil; for he gives to his beloved sleep."[10] The Sabbath, too, is God's blessing for his beloved. Like sleep, the Sabbath can break the power of pressures we often bring home from our workplace. It can keep us from souring our stomachs with the bread of anxious toil.

Much of the Sabbath's blessing lies in cultivating a Godward life of faith. If everyone else works seven days a week, and we work six, this would seem to disadvantage us. Not in God's world! The Sabbath leads us into a greater trust in God, and a deeper dependence upon him. By choosing not to work one day each week, we acknowledge God as our Provider. We commit our needs to him, and make room for him to provide for us in ways that we cannot trace to our own efforts. God's provision is a boon to us, but so is the trust that grows in our hearts.

THE SABBATH CUP: REDEMPTION

The first decanting of significance into the Sabbath cup was the Creator's joy in his creation. This is the first meaning of the Sabbath for us, as we celebrate God's pleasure in his creative work. New meaning was poured into the cup when Israel camped at the foot of Mount Sinai and Moses gave them the Ten Commandments. A nation of former slaves, wearied to the bone by their bondage, heard this life-changing message: "When the shaping of the world was complete, the Creator rested from his work. For his honor and your health, you must rest from your work one day each week, every week, for as long as you work."

Forty years later, as they were poised to enter the land of promise, the people were given the commandments a second time. The Sabbath cup was filled with new significance. This day is God's invitation to celebrate his mighty acts of liberation:

> Observe the Sabbath day, to keep it holy, as the LORD your God commanded you. Six days you shall labor and do all your work, but the seventh day is a Sabbath to the LORD your God. On it you shall not do any work, you or your son or your daughter or your male servant or your female servant, or your ox or your donkey or any of your livestock, or the sojourner who is within your gates, that your male servant and your female servant may rest as well as you. You shall remember that you were a slave in the land of Egypt, and the LORD your God brought you out from there with a mighty hand and an outstretched arm. Therefore the LORD your God commanded you to keep the Sabbath day. (Deuteronomy 5:12-15)

The rationale for Sabbath rest in Exodus is God's work in creation; in Deuteronomy it is the redemption of his people from Egypt. Together they teach us that we are fully dependent upon God – for our existence in the world, and for our salvation. God invites us to celebrate and enjoy both.

The shift from creation to redemption is significant, but what you might miss is the corresponding change from nature to history. Our lives are embedded in nature, but nothing in nature can save us from our plight. God works in history to bring us salvation. When he delivered Israel from a life of bondage in Egypt, the day they embarked on their journey to the land of promise had a date on a calendar. It passed and never came again. It is celebrated *ad perpetuam rei memoriam*,[11] but as history, not a pattern in the natural world. Keep this in mind when we get to the Sabbath and its celebration of redemption through the life, death, and resurrection of Christ.

THE SABBATH CUP: COMPASSION

When the Sabbath commandment was first given, its purpose was not to create a celebration that allowed the people of Israel to rest while servants, guests, and animals kept working: "On it you shall not do any work, you, or your son, or your daughter, your male servant, or your female servant, or your livestock, or the sojourner who is within your gates." This brings us to another decanting of Sabbath significance: It is God's invitation to join him in bringing refreshment to others in need. The Sabbath expresses God's creational intention for all, including the animals he has placed in our lives. The blessing begins but doesn't end with us. We are to be channels through which the health-giving stream of rest flows to others.

In addition to the weekly Sabbath there was a Sabbath year (every seventh),[12] and a Sabbath year of Jubilee (every 50th year, following seven Sabbath years).[13] These commands fill the Sabbath cup even more. We learn from them that the Sabbath is more than a day. It is a cultivated way of living in God's world. Sabbath is a sign. It points our hearts to God's desire to provide:

> ➤ Rest for people
> ➤ Rest for the land
> ➤ Rest for animals
> ➤ Resources for the poor
> ➤ Redemption for slaves
> ➤ Recovery of lands
> ➤ Remittance of debt
> ➤ Renewal of community

SACRED PATTERNS

These are uppermost concerns in the sacred pattern of setting aside one day in seven, one year in seven, and one year every fifty (the year of Jubilee, following seven Sabbath years) in a rhythm of life before God.

When Israel wandered from this understanding and practice of the Sabbath, the prophets called them back:

> New moon and Sabbath and the calling of convocations –
>   I cannot endure iniquity and solemn assembly.
>   Your new moons and your appointed feasts
>   my soul hates;
> they have become a burden to me;
>   I am weary of bearing them.
>   When you spread out your hands,
>   I will hide my eyes from you;
> even though you make many prayers,
>   I will not listen;
>   your hands are full of blood.
>   Wash yourselves; make yourselves clean;
>   remove the evil of your deeds from before my eyes;
> cease to do evil,
>   learn to do good;
> seek justice,
>   correct oppression;
> bring justice to the fatherless,
>   plead the widow's cause. (Isaiah 1:14-17)

(We also learn from these prophetic words that in God's view of the Sabbath, righteousness is more important than ritual, and compassion is more important than calendars. This will be important to our understanding of the Sabbath and its practice in our day.)

This vision of the Sabbath was embraced by Jesus. He walked this path. He swam in this current. It was on a Sabbath that he proclaimed the fulfillment of an ancient prophecy in his words and deeds:

> And he came to Nazareth, where he had been brought up. And as was his custom, he went to the synagogue on the Sabbath day, and he stood up to read. And the scroll of the prophet Isaiah was given to him. He unrolled the scroll and found the place where it was written,
>
> > "The Spirit of the Lord is upon me,
> >   because he has anointed me
> >   to proclaim good news to the poor.
> > He has sent me to proclaim liberty to the captives
> >   and recovering of sight to the blind,
> >   to set at liberty those who are oppressed,
> > to proclaim the year of the Lord's favor."
>
> And he rolled up the scroll and gave it back to the attendant and sat down. And the eyes of all in the synagogue were fixed on him. And he began to say to them, "Today this Scripture has been fulfilled in your hearing." (Luke 4:18-21)

This prophetic vision lay behind Jesus' controversial actions of healing on the Sabbath (controversial only because the true meaning of this sacred day had been buried under centuries of custom).

You can see the prophetic and messianic understanding of the Sabbath in the early Church and its celebration of the agape feast, with its special focus on the poor.[14] Around 200 A.D. Tertullian wrote of the Church in North Africa: "Our feast explains itself by its name. The Greeks call it agape, i.e., affection. Whatever it costs, our outlay in the name of piety is gain, since with the good things of the feast we benefit the needy . . . as it is with God himself, a peculiar respect is shown to the lowly.[15]

In their weekly pattern of life, they shared food with the poor. They distributed resources to the destitute. It was integral to their feast, and essential to their celebration of Christ's love. This was part of a larger way of living in the world. Tertullian wrote about the financial resources of Christian congregations:

> Though we have our treasure-chest, it is not made up of purchase-money, as of a religion that has its price. On the monthly day, if he likes, each puts in a small donation; but only if it be his pleasure, and only if he be able: for there is no compulsion; all is voluntary. These gifts are, as it were, piety's deposit fund. For they are not taken thence and spent on feasts, and drinking-bouts, and eating-houses, but to support and bury poor people, to supply the wants of boys and girls destitute of means and parents, and of old persons confined now to the house; such, too, as have suffered shipwreck; and if there happen to be any in the mines, or banished to the islands, or shut up in the prisons, for nothing but their fidelity to the cause of God's Church, they become the nurslings of their confession.[16]

These followers of Jesus understood the significance of the Sabbath. Imagine the difference the Church might make in the world if we embraced this again!

QUESTIONS FOR THOUGHT AND DISCUSSION

1. Discuss your understanding and practice of the Sabbath so far in your life.

2. How can you incorporate a celebration of God's creative work in your Sabbath?

3. How could a Sabbath practice impact work-related stress and anxiety in your life?

4. How would a Sabbath practice challenge you to trust God more?

5. How does the theme of compassion in this chapter challenge and inspire your practice of the Sabbath?

CHAPTER 6

JOY AT REST
SABBATH, PART 2

FALSE FILLINGS OF THE SABBATH CUP

We can try to fill the Sabbath cup with our own interests and concerns, and not God's. This is what inflamed the prophet Isaiah and brought a stinging indictment of the nation of Israel.[1] We can also attempt to fill the cup with something that pretends to be from God, but is not. Jesus called this the "tradition of men."

> At that time Jesus went through the grainfields on the Sabbath. His disciples were hungry, and they began to pluck heads of grain and to eat. But when the Pharisees saw it, they said to him, "Look, your disciples are doing what is not lawful to do on the Sabbath. He said to them . . . if you had known what this means, 'I desire mercy, and not sacrifice,' you would not have condemned the guiltless. For the Son of Man is lord of the Sabbath. He went on from there and entered their synagogue. And a man was there with a withered hand. And they asked him, "Is it lawful to heal on the Sabbath?" – so that they might accuse him. He said to them, "Which one of you who has a sheep, if it falls into a pit on the Sabbath, will not take hold of it and lift it out? Of how much more

value is a man than a sheep! So it is lawful to do good on the Sabbath." Then he said to the man, "Stretch out your hand." And the man stretched it out, and it was restored, healthy like the other. (Matthew 12:1-13)

The Pharisees and the scribes asked him, "Why do your disciples not walk according to the tradition of the elders, but eat with defiled hands?" And he said to them, "Well did Isaiah prophesy of you hypocrites, as it is written,

'This people honors me with their lips,
    but their heart is far from me;
in vain do they worship me,
    teaching as doctrines the commandments of men.'

You leave the commandment of God and hold to the tradition of   men. (Mark 7:1-8)

I understand that I will be putting myself at risk with some, but I'm willing to do that for a clearer understanding of the Sabbath. When the fourth commandment was originally given, it had nothing to do with organized religion.[2] There was no Jewish temple.[3] There were no synagogues.[4]   No formal ceremonies or rituals.   There were no churches. No church buildings. No church calendars. No church meetings. With apologies to my friends in the pastorate, the Sabbath had nothing to do with clergy. All of this is tradition developed over many centuries. Some Christians read these things back into the original command, but they weren't there.

When the Sabbath was first instituted, it would have been celebrated simply and informally by Jewish families in their homes, and with friends and neighbors in their communities. There were no "religious events" to attend, no "religious places" to go to, and no pressure to add "religious activities" to their busy week. Don't misunderstand: The addition of tradition isn't inherently wrong. If it illumines the true meaning of the Sabbath, if it helps us focus our hearts on God's design for this day, and if it enriches our celebration of it, it is good.[5] If it diverts and distracts, it is not. If it obscures, it is not. If it makes the Sabbath another busy day in our week, it is not. If it keeps us from rest and from living compassionately toward those who are in need (because we are so occupied with church activities), it is not.[6]

I am not the first to question Sabbath traditions. Jesus did. There is good reason to be cautious about adding our own customs to the Word of God and making them binding upon people. Jesus' activity on the Sabbath was iconoclastic. From what we see in the Gospels, he may have included the synagogue service as part of his Sabbath observance,[7] but we know little more about his actual practices on the Sabbath than that he was committed to works of compassion and healing. His disputes with religious leaders and his warning that it is possible to honor the accumulated "traditions of men" and lose the "word of God" should make us all wary of reading later Sabbath traditions back into God's command.

THE BRIMMING OF THE SABBATH CUP

The Sabbath cup was filled full in Christ because the Sabbath was fulfilled in him. Creation and redemption converged in the Incarnation as God stepped into the world of humanity as one of us. Jesus fulfilled God's creational intentions for humanity in his life, redeemed fallen humanity in his death, and inaugurated God's new creation in his resurrection. All of this now comes into focus in our celebration of the Sabbath. Norman Wirzba writes:

> Uniquely Christian Sabbath teaching takes us to the inner heart of
> the world's meaning, for in the incarnation of God in Christ the

whole of creation is given a renewed, redemptive focus. Just as the Sabbath represents the climax or fulfillment of creation, so too Jesus reveals what God's intentions for life have been all along. What does it mean to be a creature of God, and what are we to do with the life given us? How do we best live the life that will bring delight to God and health and peace to the whole creation?[8]

Lord of the Sabbath. Jesus claimed this title for himself.[9] It means that everything about the Sabbath must bow to him. Everything must honor him. Everything must point our hearts to him. This does not negate earlier Sabbath truths. Jesus made it clear that his aim was not to subtract but to sum.[10] But he also said that he came to inaugurate a new covenant.[11] God's presence and action in Christ in the new covenant cast light on the past and illumine the meaning of the old. The Sabbath's ancient focus on creation and Israel's deliverance from Egypt foreshadows Christ and is fulfilled in the new covenant inaugurated through his life, death, and resurrection. There is a comma after each disclosure of Sabbath truth in the past, and an exclamation point when everything about the Sabbath is fulfilled by its Lord, who invites us: "Come to me, all who labor and are heavy laden, and I will give you rest."[12]

In the old covenant, redemption was commemorated weekly on the Sabbath and annually on the Passover. In the new covenant it is memorialized in the Lord's Supper on the Lord's Day. In Israel's chapter, redemption was celebrated on the last day of the week. In the Church's chapter, it is celebrated on the first day.[13]

Are we justified in shifting the Sabbath from the last day of the week to the first? Of course, we are not the ones who made this change. It happened early in the life of the fledgling Church.[14] Are we justified in following their lead? The seeds of this calendar change had already been planted in the ancient Torah teaching on the Sabbath. We should recall the shift in rationale for the Sabbath in Exodus, with its focus on creation, to Deuteronomy and its focus on redemption. From creation to redemption. From nature to history.

Creation is God's first word to us, but if it is his last, we are in very great trouble. The cadences of creation can bring us rest; they cannot bring us salvation. The cycles of sun and moon give order to our lives, but they cannot redeem us. Only God's work in history can do that. Israel's redemption from Egypt foreshadows the supreme event in history that brought salvation not to a nation but to a world in need. When Christ rose from the dead on the first day of the week, the history of the world changed its course and moved in a new direction. Nothing could ever be the same again. Everything about the Sabbath is now relative to this.

The Sabbath cup is now full. The Sabbath is fulfilled in Christ. It drops to its knees before its Lord. We celebrate this on Sunday, the Lord's Day, the day of his resurrection, in honor of him. He is our justification for changing the day of our Sabbath.[15] He alone is worthy, and he is worthy indeed!

Creation is not left behind in our Sabbath observance. It is still essential to the story, but in a new and heightened way. The resurrection of Christ not only sealed our redemption, it inaugurated God's new creation, which will come in its fullness in the resurrection of the dead and the new heavens and the new earth. In the framework of a seven-day week, the first day signifies the beginnings of this new creation, and our part in it even now: "Therefore, if anyone is in Christ, he is a new creation. The old has passed away; behold, the new has come."[16]

Nothing is abandoned. All is fulfilled. In our Sabbath celebration we honor God's creative work and joy. We find refreshment and renewal in a weekly respite. We remember and celebrate the redemption of Israel from their plight in Egypt. We craft lives that are compassionate toward others in need because God has been compassionate to us in ours. Most importantly, we celebrate what God has done for us in Christ and what he has pledged yet to do.

THE SABBATH CUP: OVERFLOWING WITHOUT END

The Passover was a transitional meal. When it was first celebrated, Jewish families ate and drank, looking back to Egypt and their deliverance from bondage, and forward to their destination, which lay before them in the promise of God.

The words of Jesus in the Last Supper are cast in the same way. The bread and cup are memorials: "And he took bread, and when he had given thanks, he broke it and gave it to them, saying, 'This is my body, which is given for you. Do this in remembrance of me.'"[17] At the same time, they direct our hearts to the future and the fullness of God's redemptive work in Christ:

> For I tell you I will not eat it [the bread] until it is fulfilled in the kingdom of God. (Luke 22:16)

> For I tell you that from now on I will not drink of the fruit of the vine until the kingdom of God comes. (Luke 22:18)[18]

Prophetic words in both the Old Testament and the New foretell the day when Creation and Redemption will meet in the new heavens and new earth. The Curse will be undone, and all creation will be raised to new and glorious heights:

> For you shall go out in joy
>   and be led forth in peace;
> the mountains and the hills before you

shall break forth into singing,
　　and all the trees of the field shall clap their hands.
Instead of the thorn shall come up the cypress;
　　instead of the brier shall come up the myrtle;
and it shall make a name for the LORD,
　　an everlasting sign that shall not be cut off. (Isaiah 55:12-13)
For behold, I create new heavens
　　and a new earth,
and the former things shall not be remembered
　　or come into mind.
But be glad and rejoice forever
　　in that which I create;
for behold, I create Jerusalem to be a joy,
　　and her people to be a gladness.
I will rejoice in Jerusalem
　　and be glad in my people;
no more shall be heard in it the sound of weeping
　　and the cry of distress. (Isaiah 65:17-19)

For the creation waits with eager longing for the revealing of the sons of God. For the creation was subjected to futility, not willingly, but because of him who subjected it, in hope that the creation itself will be set free from its bondage to corruption and obtain the freedom of the glory of the children of God. For we know that the whole creation has been groaning together in the pains of childbirth until now. And not only the creation, but we ourselves, who have the firstfruits of the Spirit, groan inwardly as we wait eagerly for adoption as sons, the redemption of our bodies. For in this hope we were saved. (Romans 8:19-24)[19]

The Lord's Supper celebrated on the Lord's Day points to a future Sabbath and a future feast that will eclipse all others.[20] With our risen and glorified Lord in our midst, we will revel and rest in the shalom of God's Kingdom in a newly created world that will never end.[21]

QUESTIONS FOR THOUGHT AND DISCUSSION

1. Discuss the following quote in light of what you see in Christian circles that you are familiar with:

   > It is possible to fill the Sabbath cup with our own interests and concerns, and not God's. This is what inflamed the prophet Isaiah and brought a stinging indictment against the nation of Israel. But it is also possible to fill the cup with something that pretends to be from God, but is not. Jesus called this false filling, the "tradition of men."

2. Discuss the following quote and how it influences your view of the Sabbath:

   > When the fourth commandment was originally given, it had nothing to do with organized religion. Nothing. There was no Jewish temple. There were no synagogues. No formal ceremonies or rituals. There were no churches. No church buildings. No church calendars. No church meetings. (With apologies to my friends in the pastorate, the Sabbath had nothing to do with clergy!) All of this was tradition that developed over many centuries.

3. What does it mean for you to make Jesus the Lord of your Sabbath?

4. Do you think the Church has been justified in changing the Sabbath from the seventh to the first day of the week? If so; why? If not, why?

5. How does the future orientation of the Lord's Supper and the Lord's Day change the way you celebrate them? What difference does this make in the way you live in the world?

CHAPTER 7

JOY AT PLAY, PART 1

"All work and no play makes Jack a dull boy." Probably. It will surely make him a tired boy, an exhausted boy in the long run, and eventually, if it becomes a way of life, a burned-out boy. Jack will forfeit much joy that could have been his. Josef Pieper said it well:

> Work itself, when deprived of its counterparts, genuine festivity and true leisure, becomes inhuman: it may, whether endured silently or 'heroically,' become a bare, hopeless, effort, resemble the labor of Sisyphus, who in fact is the mythical paradigm of the 'Worker' chained to his labor without rest, and without inner satisfaction.[1]

We can be excessive with work or play, but in God's design both are essential beats in the tempo of life. We have explored joy at work. Where should we begin exploring joy at play?

OUR PLAYFUL GOD

Be honest: What was your first response to the title of this section? I can tell you what mine would have been for many years. I would have been skeptical. So much so, in fact, that I would have been tempted to put this book down. I might not have read further. The author would have lost credibility with me, because the notion of a playful God would have rubbed against the grain of my theological upbringing. The words might as well have been "Our Lazy God," or "Our Irresponsible God." Not that I've ever been opposed to play; it just would never have occurred to me to connect our play with God himself. It would have seemed inappropriate. Undignified. Even careless for a God who has a universe to run and a world to save. If you find yourself agreeing with those sentiments, let me encourage you to reconsider. I did and changed my mind.

Let's start with a question you might not have thought to ask: What did God do before creation? Lewis Smedes wrote:

> What did God do before he had a world to tend? He was planning hell, it has been impishly suggested, for people who ask such impertinent questions. But the question is not at all improper. The fathers who gave us the doctrine of the Trinity were really responding to the same question. Their answer was that God the Father was eternally generating the Son and that both collaborated in the generation of the Spirit. And the three of them were simply enjoying being with each other. Three persons with nothing much to do, no time schedule to keep, no superior's orders to obey, no problem of survival, and no creatures to worry about. If in some impossible fantasy we could have looked on, we might have scolded the holy Trinity for wasting time. But we would have been outsiders, unable to understand the freedom of the Trinity to have their own rules to play by. And we would have been mystified,

perhaps, by the enormous pleasure that they seemed to have in what they were doing.[2]

Tantalizing, isn't it!

Why did God create? This is another important question. The right answer can't be because he was lonely or bored, that he lost a bet and had to do it, that he did it on a dare or a whim, that he was somehow compelled to do it, or that there was a deficit in his existence that could only be made up by creating a universe. If God is supreme, none of this can be true. His life was full and complete before the first word of creation. Here is the right answer to our question: God created from the plenitude of his pleasure, for the sheer joy of creating. He created from the overflow of his everlasting delight. The universe is a surplus to him. It is "gloriously superfluous."[3]   As Smedes put it: God was "free to create or not to create. He did it out of his own good pleasure, for the divine fun of it."[4]

We are used to thinking of creation as the work of God, but there is a playful dimension, as well. In human play we bring new, imaginative worlds and scenarios into being where our games takes place. We create rules and objectives for these game-worlds that are not part of our ordinary, mundane existence (which is why play can liberate us from stressful circumstances in the world we wake up to every day). This is part of what it means to bear the image of a creative God.

Picture a game of cards. The number of cards, the value and significance of the cards, and the rules and goals of the game are all part of creative play. When we sit at a table with family or friends with these cards, these rules, and the same objective, we enter an imaginary world. When we are dealt cards and our turn comes around, we play our own parts in this creative endeavor. Our options are limited to an imaginative use of the cards we have been dealt. Now think of the possibilities before God's first creative act. Philosophers call them "logically possible worlds." In creation, there were no cards dealt to God. His play had no imposed limits. He was free to create any number of games, or worlds. Jürgen Moltmann wrote: "The creative God plays with his own possibilities and creates out of nothing that which pleases him."[5]

Behind the work of creation there is divine pleasure. Play. Fun.

If we find it difficult to include play in our understanding of God, it is because our thoughts of him are too small. Our energy and resources are always locked in a zero-sum contest. Whatever is given to play is lost to work. And there is more work to do than we have time and energy for. The result is that we feel guilty (or are made to feel guilty) for playing. But this can't be true of an Almighty God! Nothing diminishes his power. Nothing diverts his attention. Nothing distracts him. Nothing competes for his time or resources. Nothing jeopardizes the success of his plans. This is not only why God can play, it is why we can play. Because we have such a great and glorious God who has pledged himself to us, we can step away from our work and join him in his recreation.

PLAY AS WORSHIP

Before you dismiss this as theological quackery, let me introduce you to the Hebrew word *sachaq*.[6] In the Old Testament it was used of play:

> There go the ships, and Leviathan, which you formed to *play* in it. (Psalm 104:26)

> And the streets of the city will be filled with boys and girls *playing* in its streets. (Zechariah 8:5)

It was also used of singing and playing instrumental music:

> And the women sang to one another as they *celebrated*,
> "Saul has struck down his thousands,
>   and David his ten thousands." (1 Samuel 18:7)

> David and all Israel were *celebrating* before God with all their might, even with songs and with lyres, harps, tambourines, cymbals and with trumpets. (1 Chronicles 13:8)

It was often accompanied by festive dance:

> And as the ark of the covenant of the LORD came to the city of David, Michal the daughter of Saul looked out of the window and saw King David dancing and *celebrating*. (1 Chronicles 15:29)

> Again I will build you and you shall be rebuilt, O virgin of Israel! Again you adorn yourself with tambourines, and go forth in the dance of the *merrymakers*. (Jeremiah 31:4)

Did you catch the phrase about David and his fellow Israelites dancing and celebrating (playing) before God? This is worship. In fact, David insisted that it was:

> As the ark of the LORD came into the city of David, Michal the daughter of Saul looked out of the window and saw King David leaping and dancing before the LORD. . . . And David said to Michal, "It was before the LORD, who chose me above your father and above all his house, to appoint me as prince over Israel, the people of the LORD—and I will celebrate before the LORD. (2 Samuel 6:16, 21)

Before you write David off as a "vulgar fellow,"[7] as his wife did, you should know that God's appraisal of him was very different: "I have found in David the son of Jesse a man after my heart, who will do all my will."[8]   To our ancient Jewish brothers and sisters (at least those who were attuned to God), music, dance, play, and worship were woven together in the fabric of life. If play is a God-centered celebration of life, if it is animated with thanksgiving and energized by joy, God is pleased with our reverent revelry.

THE EARTH AS A PLAYGROUND

The play of children. If we could see our planet as God does, at any given time on any given day we would see millions of children playing in homes, yards, streets, fields, and parks around the world. It isn't laziness. It's what children do. Except for the fact that it often seems to get lost along the way, we might say that play is a human instinct.[9] The earth is much more than a playground, but it is that, even if we only consider the play of children.

Now picture Jesus inviting children to come to him, blessing them, and telling his adult followers that they must become like children to enter the Kingdom of God.[10] Does that exclude their playfulness? I don't think so. The play of children epitomizes health, which is why it is included in prophetic portraits of shalom in God's climactic work of redemption.[11] If anything, we should picture Jesus playing with children. Can you see him chasing them or running from them in a game of tag? Playing hide and seek? Skipping? Rolling down a hill? Carrying them on his shoulders and bouncing them on his lap? I can. I believe that you should. The loss of play is not a right of passage into the Kingdom. It may keep you from it. It will not move you closer to Jesus. It may move you farther away.

Animals at play. In the early days of spring, as I drive from our house into Boulder, Colorado where I work, I enjoy watching calves run, jump, and kick their feet into the air in nearby fields. As far as I can tell there is no goal to their gambol. It is play for the sake of play. But I know this: Their frolic always points me to their Maker and mine, and to his delight in their playful exuberance. The Scriptures celebrate this joy: "But for you who fear my name, the sun of righteousness shall rise with healing in its wings. You shall go out leaping like calves from the stall."[12]

Think about the play of animals around the world never seen by human eyes. They don't play to entertain us, so presumably they play even if we don't see them. What if they play for the entertainment and pleasure of their Maker who sees them in every moment and in every place? What if he plays with them? Before you reject this, let's look at this Psalm:

> O LORD, how manifold are your works!
> In wisdom have you made them all;
>   the earth is full of your creatures.
> Here is the sea, great and wide,
>   which teems with creatures innumerable,
>   living things both small and great.
>
> There go the ships,
>   and Leviathan, which you formed to play in it. (Psalm 104:24-26)

Leviathan in this context may have been a whale. In the original Hebrew, "which you formed to play in it" can also be translated, "which you formed to play with."[13] In either case God creates with play in mind. If the meaning of the word is *with*, then we see God playing with animals he created. Either way, you have a decision to make. You can reject these possibilities because they don't fit your understanding of God, or you can accept them as an insight into the nature of God, and let them reshape the way you think about him and the world we live in. Your choice.

You've probably had this experience: You think you know a friend. You know her well enough that you can guess what she would say and what she would do, and you are usually right. And then she reveals something about herself that you didn't know and would never have guessed. At first the revelation is unsettling. Disconcerting. It doesn't fit what you thought you knew, and you find yourself questioning whether you've been told the truth with this new information. But when you let the self-disclosure sink in, it begins to cast new light on your friendship. It clarifies. It explains. It makes sense. In fact it gives you a new understanding and a greater appreciation of your friend. Are you open to that possibility with God?

THE SIGNIFICANCE OF PLAY

Those who don't play, and even those who do, are likely to miss the significance of play in a God-centered vision of life. Robert Johnston writes:

> The evidence for "play" in the Bible is extensive. Yet we have for the most part failed to recognize it or act upon it because our work-dominated culture has biased our interpretation. . . . We have mistakenly interpreted the Song of Songs to be about God's love for his people, unable to consider that it could actually be a song in praise of lovers at play. We have limited the Sabbath to that necessary pause that refreshes, failing to understand its prior rationale as reflecting the pattern of God himself. We have failed to note the playful counterpoint that festival and feasting, music and dance provided – and are meant to provide. . . . We have failed to see their function to be that of surprising us with joy. . . . As Christians we have failed to let Scripture speak authoritatively to us about our need to play.[14]

We need play, but not as we need food and drink. It is deeper than that. God doesn't eat or drink, but he does play! Play connects us with God, and this is our greatest need. Here we find our greatest joy. This is play's true significance.

PLAY AND THE SABBATH

"If we spend the Lord's day in making good cheer, and in playing and gaming, is that a good honoring of God? No, is it not a mockery . . . and a very unhallowing of his name?"[15] Many Christians frown at the idea of playing on the Sabbath. I will try to put you in a position to reach your own conclusion about this, but my primary interest is exploring the Sabbath and play to see what we can learn from their kinship.

Let's begin by retracing some of our steps in the last two chapters. First, the Sabbath limits work in our lives. Play does this, too. If you are resting you are not working. If you are playing you are not working. Both remind us that while work is important, it is not ultimate. God is. The Sabbath is like play:

> The Sabbath is meant as a time of rest from the world – a period of non-work and delight in which one's "useless" activity both fosters a recognition of the divine and sanctifies and refreshes ongoing life. Described this way, the Sabbath can be understood as analogous to, if not paradigmatic of, play. . . . The Sabbath, as "play," is that parenthesis in life which has its rightful limits. Nonproductive in design, it nevertheless has significant value for its participants. Entered into freely and joyfully, it has rules and order for the sake of its integrity. . . . Lastly, this "play" of the Sabbath frees one up more generally for a "playful" life-style. One's six days of work are transformed and put into perspective by the Sabbath experience.[16]

Second, the purpose of the Sabbath is not simply time away from work, it is a "Sabbath to the Lord," which means that he is to be the focus of the day. The play I am interested in shares this vision. It is a celebration of life *coram Deo*.[17]

Third, the Sabbath is an occasion for reveling in God's goodness in creation, bringing with it the refreshment of thanksgiving and praise.

Godward play can do this, too. You may not be able to compose a theological treatise while you are playing, but offering the pleasures of play to God with a thankful heart is not a distraction. If you can walk and think at the same time, you can do this. The only requirement is being attentive and intentional.

Fourth, habituating our lives in a healthy Sabbath pattern allows us to break the power of anxious toil during our work week: "It is vain that you rise up early and go late to rest, eating the bread of anxious toil; for he gives to his beloved sleep." We could also say, "He gives his beloved play." Like sleep, and like the Sabbath, play can save us from our stress, and rescue us from the worries of work.

Fifth, as we saw in the last chapter, when the Sabbath command was originally given, it had nothing to do with organized religion. The day was not filled with "religious places" to go to and "religious events" to attend. Most of it was observed by families in their homes, and with neighbors and friends. Godward play often looks like this.

The prophets reminded people of the true meaning and purpose of the Sabbath, and the ways in which they had wandered from that path. Listen again to the words of the Lord through Isaiah:

> New moon and Sabbath and the calling of convocations—
>   I cannot endure iniquity and solemn assembly.
>   Your new moons and your appointed feasts
>   my soul hates;
> they have become a burden to me;
>   I am weary of bearing them.
>   When you spread out your hands,
>   I will hide my eyes from you;
> even though you make many prayers,
>   I will not listen;
>   your hands are full of blood.

Wash yourselves; make yourselves clean;
    remove the evil of your deeds from before my eyes;
cease to do evil,
    learn to do good;
seek justice,
    correct oppression;
bring justice to the fatherless,
    plead the widow's cause. (Isaiah 1:14-17)

Not all that had become religious tradition was compatible with the Sabbath. Not all play is consonant with the Sabbath either. Let's review the word of God through Isaiah:

If you turn back your foot from the Sabbath,
    from doing your pleasure on my holy day,
and call the Sabbath a delight
    and the holy day of the LORD honorable;
if you honor it, not going your own ways,
    or seeking your own pleasure, or talking idly;
then you shall take delight in the LORD,
    and I will make you ride on the heights of the earth;
I will feed you with the heritage of Jacob your father,
    for the mouth of the LORD has spoken. (Isaiah 58:13-14)

If our play is the pursuit of our own pleasure (self-interest, self-gratification, selfish ambition), it deviates from the purpose of the Sabbath and dishonors it. If our play asserts our own way in life and does not embrace God's, it profanes this holy day. If it is the moral equivalent of talking idly, if it is frivolous (without purpose) or lazy (avoiding work rather than resting from work), it cannot enjoy his blessing. It insults the Sabbath.

But what if our play celebrates the Creator and his creative work? What if it draws our hearts to him in thanksgiving and praise? What if we enjoy

God's gift of play, and we offer it to him as an act of worship? What if it reflects trust in God in our conscious choice not to work for that time? What if it energizes us? What if it refreshes us for our work? What if it enables us to flourish in life more than we otherwise would? What if life for us includes not only play, but justice and mercy, and we pursue it all with passion? Is this play compatible with the Sabbath? Yes! God himself joins us in our recreation!

The disapproval of play on the Sabbath at the beginning of this section was written by the great reformer, John Calvin. But I should also let you know that there is a long-standing story that when John Knox, a fellow reformer from Scotland, visited Calvin, he found him lawn bowling with friends on a Sabbath.[18] I will let Calvin scholars argue about the historicity of the tale, and how, if it is true, it fits into his theological development. I don't know what your conclusion about play on the Sabbath will be, but I can tell you that if the story is authentic, knowing what I do about the true intent of the Sabbath and what I know about this "God-intoxicated man,"[19] I would have joined him in the game and thanked God for the playful opportunity.

QUESTIONS FOR THOUGHT AND DISCUSSION

1. What was your first reaction to the words "Our Playful God"? What are the obstacles to connecting play with God in your thoughts of him?

2. What difference does it make to you to see creation as divine play?

3. Discuss this quote:

   > To our ancient Jewish brothers and sisters (at least those who were attuned to God), music, dance, play, and worship were woven together in the fabric of life. If play is a God-centered celebration of life as a good gift, if it is animated with thanksgiving and energized by joy, God is pleased with our reverent revelry.

4. Talk about the play of children and the play of animals and how that should factor into your understanding of play in a Christian vision of life.

5. Talk about the kinship between the Sabbath and play. Would you have joined John Calvin in a game of lawn bowling on the Sabbath? If not, why not? If so, why?

CHAPTER 8

JOY AT PLAY, PART 2

W e should not idealize play. Though it is a good gift from God, like everything else in this fallen world, and everything else we touch, it can be perverted. It can be corrupted. It can become an idol. It can be antithetical to the purposes of our Creator. When that happens, we are not only wasting time in our play, we are wasting life. We cheapen a good gift. If we do not take our play seriously (not to be mistaken for somberly or solemnly), it becomes frivolous. There is no virtue or joy in it. C.S. Lewis wrote, "Our leisure, even our play, is a matter of serious concern. There is no neutral ground in the universe: every square inch, every split second, is claimed by God and counterclaimed by Satan. . . . It is a serious matter to choose wholesome recreations."[1]

Frivolous play is the favorite pastime of our generation. Play is trivialized by self-centeredness and self-indulgence. For some, play is only amusement. For others it is a way of avoiding responsibilities, whether it is work or relational commitments in marriage and family. Even for those who profess faith in God, many play without a thought of him in their heads or affection for him in their hearts. If it is not included in our worship and enjoyment of God, play falls short of its intended role in our lives.

PLAY AS A PRELUDE TO JOY

Play can open our hearts to joy. There are good reasons for this. First, whether the Giver of the gift is acknowledged or not, play is possible because of the goodness of creation, and behind it, the goodness of our Creator. Play links us to this. Second, play connects us with a playful God and his design for life in his world. If it is wholesome, he joins us in our play! Third, all healthy pleasure points to joy. In *Path of Life* I wrote:

> If you were to ask the question "What is joy?" of the ancient Scriptures of the Jewish people, the answer you would discover is that joy is a kind of pleasure.[2] You would learn, perhaps to your surprise, that sacred prophets, poets, and historians alike esteemed it as the highest and best of all the pleasures of life, and the one Pleasure that embraces, enhances, and enlarges all other pleasures given by God.[3]

This includes the pleasures of play. By their very nature, playful pleasures point beyond themselves to joy, where they find their true fulfillment. They are transposed by joy. Joy takes them up and into its song. The fourth reason we will explore in what follows.

PLAY, SHALOM, AND THE COMING KINGDOM

Nicholas Wolterstorff describes shalom as a "a peace which at its highest is enjoyment. To dwell in shalom is to enjoy living before God, to enjoy living in nature, to enjoy living with one's fellows, to enjoy life with oneself."[4] When Eden is restored and raised to even greater heights in the resurrection and the new heavens and new earth, we will know the shalom of God in its fullness. It is pictured in these prophetic words:

They shall come and sing aloud on the height of Zion,
  And they shall be radiant over the goodness of the LORD,
Over the grain, the wine, and the oil,
  And over the young of the flock and the herd;
Their life shall be like a watered garden,
  And they shall languish no more.
Then shall the young women rejoice in the dance,
  And the young men and the old shall be merry.
(Jeremiah 31:12-13)

This is a description of play. It is life at its highest and best before God. One day it will be ours in ways that we have barely glimpsed.

Martin Luther wrote that in the resurrection people will "play with heaven and earth, the sun and all the creatures." And "All creatures shall have their fun, love and joy and shall laugh with thee and thou with them."[5] (There it is again – God playing with his creatures!) As a sign of wholeness and well-being, play anticipates this eschatological shalom and realizes it in part. In ways that we miss more often than not, play not only connects us with deep realities in the world, but with God's plan for the ages.

PLAY AND SPORTS

I don't have anything to say about professional sports here. I'm a fan, but I see this as work for these athletes.[6] It should be explored in that context.[7] Nor do I have anything to say about athletic competition as a path to a professional career. (As a little league baseball coach I was dismayed to watch some parents push their children in this direction even at an early age.) What I have in mind is the play of an amateur.[8] Sports for the love of the game. Sports for the sheer pleasure they bring.

JOY AT PLAY, PART 2

Devout Jews in antiquity didn't participate in athletic games and didn't frequent pagan gymnasia. Athletic competition in the Greek and Roman eras took place in the buff. Games were dedicated to the gods.[9] Neither was permissible for people of Jewish faith. Nevertheless, from the sacred writings they left we can see that the ancient Jewish people admired and celebrated physical prowess and strength:

> In [the heavens] he has set a tent for the sun,
> which comes out like a bridegroom leaving his chamber,
> and, like a strong man, runs its course with joy. (Psalm 19:4-5)

> For who is God, but the LORD?
> And who is a rock, except our God?
>   the God who equipped me with strength
>   and made my way blameless.
> He made my feet like the feet of a deer
>   and set me secure on the heights.
> He trains my hands for war,
>   so that my arms can bend a bow of bronze. (Psalm 18:31-34)

The New Testament often uses athletic metaphors to express truths about discipleship and Christian living:

> I appeal to you, brothers, by our Lord Jesus Christ and by the love of the Spirit, to strive together with me in your prayers to God on my behalf. (Romans 15:30)

> Do you not know that in a race all the runners run, but only one receives the prize? So run that you may obtain it. Every athlete exercises self-control in all things. They do it to receive a perishable wreath, but we an imperishable. So I do not run aimlessly; I do not box as one beating the air. But I discipline my body and keep it under control, lest after preaching to others I myself should be disqualified. (1 Corinthians 9:24-27)

Only let your manner of life be worthy of the gospel of Christ, so that whether I come and see you or am absent, I may hear of you that you are standing firm in one spirit, with one mind striving side by side for the faith of the gospel. (Philippians 1:27)

Not that I have already obtained this or am already perfect, but I press on to make it my own, because Christ Jesus has made me his own. Brothers, I do not consider that I have made it my own. But one thing I do: forgetting what lies behind and straining forward to what lies ahead, I press on toward the goal for the prize of the upward call of God in Christ Jesus. (Philippians 3:12-14)[10]

Sports are part of our "embeddedness in the physical creation."[11] Whether it is throwing a ball, running on a track or a court, swimming in a pool, skiing down a mountain, or surfing the waves of an ocean, the physicality of the venue and the strength, agility, balance, coordination, and endurance required in sports are all part of the world that God created and pronounced good.[12]

The Ultimate Fan. It is not irreverent to think of God as the ultimate sports enthusiast.[13] He admires the gifts he gives and enjoys seeing them put to their intended use. I don't know if he takes sides. I think it more likely that he applauds all teams and all athletes. He cheers for both sides in a competition, like a parent with children on opposing teams. When my children were young, I enjoyed watching them create competitive contests with neighborhood friends. I cheered them all when they did well, and encouraged them when they did not. If I who am evil can do this, how much more our Father in Heaven![14] There is no greater fan than our God.

Stewarding God's gifts. "Every good gift is from God."[15] This includes physical talents and abilities, and sports as the arena in which these gifts are used. God delights in the gifts he gives and enjoys our pleasure in them. They bring joy to the Giver and to the gifted. We are responsible for stewarding

God's gifts. Athletes do this through sporting events and rigorous preparation for them. They steward their talents through discipline, strenuous effort, pushing themselves to their limits, overcoming obstacles, and setting and accomplishing goals. In team sports stewardship includes cooperation, communication, and coordinating the skills of all. A game plan is an exercise in stewardship: strategizing how best to put talents to use in competitive situations.

"As iron sharpens iron, so one man sharpens another."[16] There are many ways in which this happens in our lives. In sports it takes place in formal competition and in practice sessions where skills are honed, strategies are refined, mistakes are corrected, under-performance is reproved, and excellence is cheered. Even if someone wins and someone loses in a competitive event, in a vision of sports illumined by Christ, competition is not about conquest. A contest creates an opportunity for me to move closer to the goal of being the best athlete I can be. Fellow contestants provide the occasion for self-improving competition. By bringing my best to a competitive event, I serve my fellow competitor (and thus fulfill the command to love my neighbor as myself) by helping him become the best he can be. If he plays well, I congratulate him; if not, I hope better for him next time. In either event, I thank him for helping me become a better athlete.

As we think of becoming the best we can be, we should note parallels between moral virtue and athletic virtue.[17] The best athletes are known for single-mindedness, discipline, commitment, collegiality, cooperation, and collaboration. Modeling and heroism are important to both moral and athletic virtue. Mentoring and coaching are indispensable to both. Community is vital to both. In turn, sports develop community through group participation, common values, common commitments, and common objectives. If people learn to live well in this community, the skills they acquire can be fruitful in other social settings.

Deo Gloria. God is surely not glorified by much that is true of sports in our day: self-aggrandizement, commercialism, hero worship, cult-like devotion to teams, a false religion of success, winning at any cost, triumphalism, cheating, exploitation, anger, intentional injury of others, and parental abuse of children, coaches, umpires, and referees. The list of evils is much longer. However, similar charges could be laid at the feet of workplaces, art galleries, dance studios, and concert halls – wherever human egos in their fallenness shape the use of God's gifts.

While we must acknowledge the potential for evil, we should also recognize Christian athletes who are counter-cultural in their sport, who devote their athletic gifts to the glory of God, and enjoy them as his good gifts. For every one who does this in the public eye there are thousands who quietly enjoy their sport and experience great pleasure as they push themselves to their limits to become the best they can be at what they do. Their motivation is not applause in the stands, but pleasure in their sport and the praise of their God. The glory is God's, the joy is theirs, and the appreciation is ours when we watch and cheer them on.

Athletic joy. This joy has several facets. There is pleasure in physical fitness. Delight in strength and speed, in agility and balance. There is joy in camaraderie and community among teammates and fellow athletes. There is pleasure in the rush that comes with intense physical exertion and the thrill of competition and victory.

In *Path of Life* I wrote:

> Aristotle taught that pleasure is the perfection of an activity. Every activity has a pleasure that is suitable to it, that is, which arises from the action itself. We talk about this kind of pleasure when we say that we enjoy doing something. Intellectual pleasures arise from intellectual pursuits. Aesthetic pleasures arise from artistic pursuits.[18]

The same is true of athletic activity. There is a pleasure in accomplishment. A delight in performing well. A joy in giving your very best. And there is pleasure in the sport itself, as the Psalmist wrote of the strong man who runs his course with joy,[19] and as Olympic champion and missionary Eric Liddell famously said of God and running, "He made me fast, and when I run I feel his pleasure."

I will never know the pleasure of creating art with my hands, but I enjoy knowing that my artistic friends do. I enjoy their gifts. Nor will everyone experience athletic joy. But for those who do, it is exhilarating! It is a good gift from our good God.

QUESTIONS FOR THOUGHT AND DISCUSSION

1. How do you see the Fall impacting play in our culture?

2. Discuss this quote in its context: "Even in our fallen world, play can open our hearts to joy."

3. If God is the giver of every good and perfect gift, how does this impact your view of sports and stewardship?

4. Discuss this quote:

   As we think of becoming the best we can be, we should note parallels between moral virtue and athletic virtue. The best athletes are known for single-mindedness, discipline, commitment, collegiality, cooperation, and collaboration. Modeling and heroism are important to both moral and athletic virtue. Mentoring and coaching are indispensable to both. Community is vital to both.

5. Review the section "Athletic Joy" and talk about your own experiences if you play sports. If you don't, does this help you appreciate the experience of athletes?

ABOUT THE AUTHOR

In 1983 Rick and Sue Howe moved to Boulder, Colorado, where they raised three children – Amberle, Lorien, and Jamison – and have devoted more than thirty years to campus ministry at the University of Colorado. In addition to writing and speaking, Rick now leads University Ministries, whose mission is to "inspire and nurture a thoughtful pursuit of Christ, one student, one professor, one university at a time." To learn more about Rick, visit his website at www.rickhowe.org. You can also follow him on Facebook at *Rick Howe on Joy* and on Twitter @rickhoweonjoy. To learn more about University Ministries, see www.university-ministries.org.

ENDNOTES

PREFACE

1 Proverbs 17:22

2 Dallas Willard, *Renovation of the Heart: Putting on the Character of Christ* (Colorado Springs, CO: NavPress, 2002), p. 133.

3 Peter Kreeft, *Heaven: The Heart's Deepest Longing* (San Francisco: Ignatius Press, Expanded Edition, 1980), p. 129.

CHAPTER 1 JOY AT WORK: CREATION

1 See:

> The earth is the LORD's and the fullness thereof,
>   the world and those who dwell therein.
> for he has founded it upon the seas
>   and established it upon the rivers. (Psalm 24:1-2)

2 Psalm 104:31

3 Nicholas Wolterstorff, *Art in Action: Toward a Christian Aesthetic* (Grand Rapids, MI: William B. Eerdmans Publishing Co., 1980), p. 69.

4 The Hebrew word translated "created" in this text is the verb *bara'* – the same word used of God's work in the Genesis account.

5 John 5:17

6 See:

> Then God said, "Let us make man in our image, after our likeness. And let them have dominion over the fish of the sea and over the birds of the heavens and over the livestock and over all the earth and over every creeping thing that creeps on the earth."
>
> > So God created man in his own image,
> >   in the image of God he created him;
> >   male and female he created them. (Genesis 1:26-27)

7 It is often the case that theologians are right in what they affirm and wrong in what they deny. If we begin with the premise that the image of God is multifaceted, we can affirm valuable insights without choosing sides in theological debate. I would say that just as marriage is consequential to the relational dimension of the image of God in us, work is consequential to the "dominion dimension" of God's image in us.

8   Alan Richardson denies that there is an analogy between God's work and ours: "The Bible does not speak of man's work as 'creative', or suggest that there is any real analogy between the 'work' of God and the work of men." Alan Richardson, *The Biblical Doctrine of Work* (London: SCM Press LTD, p. 11.

We must qualify the analogy, but surely it is given to us in the fourth commandment:

> Remember the Sabbath day, to keep it holy. Six days you shall labor, and do all your work, but the seventh day is a Sabbath to the LORD your God. On it you shall not do any work, you, or your son, or your daughter, your male servant, or your female servant, or your livestock, or the sojourner who is within your gates. For in six days the LORD made heaven and earth, the sea, and all that is in them, and rested on the seventh day. Therefore the LORD blessed the Sabbath day and made it holy. (Exodus 20:8-11)

9   While I acknowledge that contemporary genetic evidence and other postulates of evolutionary theory represent a challenge that should engage Christians in serious thinking and dialogue, I did not come to my belief (nor will I abandon my belief) in a historical Adam and Eve, an original Edenic environment in which they lived, and a state of innocence from which they fell, on the basis of scientific inquiry.

The Scriptures are the "norming norm" for my faith. I make no apologies for this. Indeed, it is a great joy to me! Having said this, the ancient texts of Scripture must be read first – as much as possible – with their original audience in mind. We should resist the temptation of importing our interests and concerns into the way we understand them, and forcing them to take up arms in our conflicts.

I recognize that the Hebrew word *adam* was used for humanity as a whole as well as for an individual in the Genesis story (Adam = Mankind). I can also see how Israel, in its exile from the promised land, would have seen itself in Adam and his expulsion from the Garden (Adam = Israel). Neither of these observations, however, negates the possibility that Adam was also viewed as a historical figure. (Compare Jacob = Israel.) Neither seems to factor into the canonical context of Jesus' teaching on marriage and divorce in Matthew 19, and Paul's exposition of redemptive history in Romans 5 – both of which posit a historical Adam.

While Jesus does not refer to an original pair by name, his affirmation of the Creator's original intention for marriage clearly has the Edenic couple in mind. ("He who created them from the beginning made them male and female, and said, 'Therefore a man shall leave his father and his mother and hold fast to his wife, and the two shall become one flesh.'" On the matter of divorce, he affirms an original state of innocence from which humanity has lapsed ("From the beginning it was not so.")

In Romans 5, Israel as a nation is not in view, and "the one man" (Adam) is distinguished from all who followed from him ("all men"). In this passage we do observe the Jewish penchant for seeing deeper meanings in their stories. Adam is not an archetype for humanity or for Israel, however, but a "type" of Christ. This is the frame of reference in which we should pursue our interpretation. The parallels are between two men (Adam and Christ), sin entering the world through one and grace through the other, an act of disobedience and an act of righteousness, judgment and justification, death and eternal life. Any other frame of reference is alien to the context. In a grand metanarrative, Paul lays out the themes of Creation, Fall, and Redemption: one man in the beginning from whom humanity sprang and through whose "act of disobedience" sin entered the world, a historical period ("from Adam to Moses"), and God's saving action through the one man, Jesus Christ ("the one who was to come").

I affirm that there is great value in the scientific enterprise, and believe that if we love God with our minds (in fulfillment of the greatest commandment) we will boldly declare that all truth is his – wherever it is found – and we will pursue it to the best of our abilities under God. I also affirm the priority and supremacy of the Scriptures for our faith, and what seems to me to be the clear teaching of Jesus and Paul. This leads me to a confident belief that whatever we may say about the age of the universe and the development of life on our planet, there was an original couple who bore the image of God without flaw, were placed in an Edenic setting of innocence, fell from that state through a primal act of disobedience, and brought sin into the world as well as all future generations of humans who fallibly bear the image of God.

For a contemporary discussion, see Matthew Barrett and Ardel B. Caneday, eds. *Four Views on the Historical Adam* (Grand Rapids: Zondervan, 2013).

[10]   See:

> He determines the number of the stars;
>   he gives to all of them their names." (Psalm 147:4)

> Lift up your eyes on high and see:
>   who created these?
> He who brings out their host by number,
>   calling them all by name,
> by the greatness of his might,
>   and because he is strong in power
>   not one is missing. (Isaiah 40:26)

[11]   Here we first see the sanctity of intellectual work as well as manual labor. Adam did both.

[12]   Genesis 2:15

[13]   See:

> The earth is the LORD's and the fullness thereof;
>   the world and all who dwell in it. (Psalm 24:1)

> The heavens are yours; the earth also is yours;
>   the world and all that is in it, you have founded them. (Psalm 89:11)

[14]   For some, this is the image of God in us. In my view, the imago is multi-faceted, and includes humans as workers (*homo faber*). The cultural mandate is given to us in this role.

15 For instance, in the dialogue, Phaedo, Plato has Socrates say, "Nothing makes a thing beautiful but the presence and participation of beauty in whatever way or manner obtained . . . I stoutly contend that by beauty all beautiful things become beautiful. Plato, "Phaedo" in *Five Great Dialogues*, trans. B. Jowett, ed., Louise Ropes Loomis (New York: Walter J. Black, Inc., 1969), p. 138. See also Paul Edwards, ed., *The Encyclopedia of Philosophy* (New York: Macmillan Publishing Co., Inc., & The Free Press, 1967), Volume Six, pp. 320-324.

16 C.S. Lewis saw them as facets of God's glory: "I was learning the far more secret doctrine that pleasures are shafts of the glory as it strikes our sensibility. As it impinges on our will or our understanding, we give it different names -- goodness or truth or the like." C.S. Lewis, *Letters to Malcolm: Chiefly on Prayer* (New York: Harcourt Brace Jovanovich, Inc., 1963), p. 89.

17 "Oh, taste and see that the LORD is good!" (Psalm 34:8)

18 2 Timothy 2:13

19 When philosophers say that God is a "necessary being," they mean that he cannot not be. If he exists, he must exist. He cannot cease to exist.

CHAPTER 2 JOY AT WORK: FALL

1 Henry Van Til wrote: "Work, then, is not a result of sin and a hindrance to man's joy, but it is the substance of his service to God, which is man's chief joy." Henry R. Van Til, *The Calvinistic Concept of Culture* (Grand Rapids, MI: Baker Book House Company, 1972), p. 221.

2 I must acknowledge that as I wrote these words, I was imagining Shelob, the great spider of Cirith Ungol, in Tolkien's classic work. See J.R.R. Tolkien, "Shelob's Lair," *The Two Towers: Being the Second Part of The Lord of the Rings* (Boston, New York: Houghton Mifflin Co., 1982)

3 "The fool says in his heart, 'There is no God.'" (Psalm 14:1; 53:1)

4 This was the view of the 18th century philosopher, Thomas Hobbes. See his *The Leviathan* (Amherst, NY: Prometheus Books, 1988). More recently it has become popular through the works of Ayn Rand. See her collection of essays, *The Virtue of Selfishness: A New Concept of Egoism* (New York, NY: Signet, 1964) and her novel, *Atlas Shrugged* (New York, NY: Penguin Group, 1999). Rand refers to her version of egoism as "rational egoism," the view that selfishness or self-interest as a guiding principle should always accord with reason.

5 The famous line, "Nature, red in tooth and claw," is from Alfred, Lord Tennyson, "In Memoriam":

Who trusted God was love indeed
And love Creation's final law–
Tho' Nature, red in tooth and claw
With ravine, shriek'd against his creed–

Thomas Hobbes had earlier expressed similar views of humanity in its natural state, in "a war of all against all," and of human life as "solitary, poor, nasty, brutish, and short." See his *The Leviathan* (Amherst, NY: Prometheus Books, 1988).

6   You might argue that cooperation is another way of getting what you want, but only if cooperation serves your interests. If you are an ethical egoist, the interests of others are not your moral concern, except as they serve your own, unless they are a means to your own ends. If you are open and transparent about this with your co-workers, you are likely to alienate them – which is why I say that coercion or duplicity are the tools an ethical egoist must use to accomplish their ends.

7   According to philosopher Rem Edwards, here are three commitments that are essential to normative hedonism:

> Pleasure, or happiness defined in terms of pleasure, is the only thing which is intrinsically good; and pain, or unhappiness defined in terms of pain, is the only thing which is intrinsically evil.
>
> Happiness, hedonistically defined, consists of a positive surplus of pleasure over pain through an extended period of time; unhappiness, hedonistically defined, consists of a surplus of pain over pleasure through an extended period of time.
>
> I ought to act to maximize pleasure or happiness and to minimize pain or unhappiness.

Rem B. Edwards, *Pleasures and Pains: A Theory of Qualitative Hedonism* (Ithaca, NY: Cornell University Press, 1979), p. 19.

8   One of the things that is destroying our economy and our culture is maximal profits measured by quarterly profit-and-loss reports. Companies no longer take the long view of profit. Long-term profitability is sacrificed for short-term success. This makes hedonism even more destructive.

9   Hedonists in the lower echelons of the corporate world use companies in their own pursuit of pleasure and avoidance of pain; it's just that they have fewer resources to accomplish their ends.

10   St. Thomas Aquinas: *Philosophical Texts*, ed. and trans. Thomas Gilby (Durham, North Carolina: The Labyrinth Press, 1982), p. 275.

11   Greed motivates economic activity, but does not ensure wealth. Exploitation has to do with the way one treats others. It is a means to an end, but does not guarantee that the end achieved will be prosperity. This is why these vices are not class-specific. They are relational vices that grow from the soil of an unhealthy valuing of money and possessions – whether one has these things in abundance or not.

[12] Adam Smith, in his classic work, *The Wealth of Nations*, famously wrote: "It is not from the benevolence of the butcher, the brewer, or the baker, that we expect our dinner, but from their regard to their own interest. We address ourselves, not to their humanity but to their self-love, and never talk to them of our own necessities but of their advantages." Adam Smith, *The Wealth of Nations* (New York, NY: Random House, 1937). p.14.

[13] Smith wrote:

> Every individual necessarily labors to render the annual revenue of the society, as great as he can. He generally, indeed, neither intends to promote the public interest, nor knows how much he is promoting it . . . he intends only his own gain, and he is in this, as in many other cases, led by an invisible hand to promote an end which was no part of his intention. Nor is it always the worse for the society that it was no part of it. By pursuing his own interest he frequently promotes that of the society more effectually than when he really intends to promote it.

Ibid., p. 423. Free enterprise is amazing in its ability to create wide-scale opportunity. My complaint is not with this system. If it were motivated by joy and not by greed, it would be unrivaled among economic systems.

[14] Norman Wirzba writes:

> In a condition of fear and distrust, we are tempted to amass as much power and possessions for ourselves as possible, believing the more control we have over our own fate and those of others the more secure we will be. This is the path of violence, the way that leads to the oppression and abuse of others.

Wirzba, *Living the Sabbath: Discovering the Rhythms of Rest and Delight*, (Grand Rapids, Michigan: Brazos Press, 2006), p. 39.

[15] None of this is meant as a judgment of capitalism per se, but of greed as its motivating force.

[16] Robert Bellah and his colleagues explore this cultural shift. See Robert N. Bellah, Richard Madsen, William M. Sullivan, Ann Swidler, and Steven M. Tipton, *Habits of the Heart: Individualism and Commitment in American Life* (New York: Harper & Row, 1986).

[17] Norman Wirzba writes:

> It is important to distinguish vocation from career, not because careers are inherently evil but because they often lack the inspiration and direction of a larger social and divine purpose. A career is an occupation we hope will bring the greatest amount of personal satisfaction and benefit. . . . When work is reduced to careerism, its divine dimension and intention are cut off. The inevitable consequence is the distortion of humanity and creation.

Wirzba, *Living the Sabbath*, p. 93.

[18] In this vision of life, we are defined by our work and our place in the workforce. We are *homo faber*: man the worker. This was an essential feature of Marxism in the nineteenth

and twentieth centuries. Capitalism may have won the contest with that philosophy, but the real winner was the underlying belief that the human project is fundamentally about work and the workplace. (What is one of the first things we ask when we meet someone? "What do you do?" "What's your line of work?" It is more than a conversation starter. We have come to identify ourselves and our worth, and to identify others and estimate their worth, by work.) Careerism is just one expression of this vision of life.

The notion of a career has created a virtual caste system in our culture: a lower caste, those who merely work, and a higher caste, those who have a career. If you have the misfortune of being in the lower caste, you do the work that makes it possible for the higher caste to pursue and enjoy a career. It becomes a way of making social distinctions and assigning value to people. It is not the only way that fallen people do this, but it has become a popular way of doing it in our day.

[19] Many now enter marriage with the provision that the relationship must not stand in the way of career goals. Couples divorce because marriage becomes an impediment to career objectives. Children are often secondary to careers, postponed until a professional status has been secured, and then consigned to surrogate parents in pre-school and daycare centers for the sake of their parents' personal advancement in the workplace.

[20] This is not to say that if you see your work as a calling from God, and a stewardship of opportunities given by him, you will not seek to be the best you can be in your work, or that you will not move from one place to another in your work. These things will be shaped, however, by a different set of values and priorities (the glory of God and the good of your family), and that makes a very big difference!

[21] We will explore the notion of calling, or vocation, in Chapter 4.

[22] The power of joy can break any addiction, including workaholism. If we are joyful people, other things are also true about us: There is a harmony between our desires and our deeds, a concord between our affections and our actions, and a congeniality between our hearts and God's. The joy of the Lord becomes our strength (Nehemiah 8:10), and no addiction is stronger than that. See the chapter "The Joyful Heart" in Rick Howe, *Path of Life: Finding the Joy You've Always Longed For* (Boulder, CO: University Ministries Press, 2017).

[23] Dorothy Sayers wrote, "Work is not, primarily, a thing one does to live, but the thing one lives to do. It is, or it should be, the full expression of the worker's faculties, the thing in which he finds spiritual, mental and bodily satisfaction, and the medium in which he offers himself to God. Dorothy Sayers, *Why Work?* A Pdf version found at: http://centerforfaithandwork.com/article/why-work-dorothy-sayers.

[24] Man the worshiper.

[25] Peter Kreeft, *Heaven: The Heart's Deepest Longing* (San Francisco: Ignatius Press, Expanded edition, 1980), p. 21.

26   What C.S. Lewis wrote of love is true anything that becomes a substitute for the true God: "Love, having become a god, becomes a demon." C.S. Lewis, *The Four Loves* (San Diego, New York, London: Harcourt Brace Jovanovich Publishers, 1960), p. 83.

Here is the biblical foundation for seeing the demonic behind false gods:

> They sacrificed to demons that were no gods, to gods they had never known, to new gods that had come recently, whom your fathers had never dreaded. (Deuteronomy 32:17)

> They sacrificed their sons and their daughters to the demons. (Psalm106:37)

> No, I imply that what pagans sacrifice they offer to demons and not to God. I do not want you to be participants with demons. (1 Corinthians 10:20)

CHAPTER 3: JOY AT WORK: REDEMPTION, PART 1

1   C.S. Lewis wrote:

> If you read history you will find that the Christians that did most for the present world were those who thought most of the next. The apostles themselves, who set out on foot to convert the Roman Empire, the great men who built up the Middle Ages, the English evangelicals who abolished the slave trade, all left their mark on earth, precisely because their minds were occupied with heaven. It is since Christians have largely ceased to think of the other world that they have become so ineffective in this one. Aim at heaven and you will get earth "thrown in." Aim at earth and you will get neither.

C.S. Lewis, *Mere Christianity* (New York: Simon & Schuster, 1996), p. 119.

2   Matthew 6:11

3   See:

> In the evening quail came up and covered the camp, and in the morning dew lay around the camp. And when the dew had gone up, there was on the face of the wilderness a fine, flake-like thing, fine as frost on the ground. When the people of Israel saw it, they said to one another, 'What is it?' For they did not know what it was. And Moses said to them, 'It is the bread that the LORD has given you to eat. This is what the LORD has commanded: 'Gather of it, each one of you, as much as he can eat. You shall each take an omer, according to the number of the persons that each of you has in his tent.' And the people of Israel did so. They gathered, some more, some less. But when they measured it with an omer, whoever gathered much had nothing left over, and whoever gathered little had no lack. Each of them gathered as much as he could eat. (Exodus 16:13-18)

4   See:

> The LORD God took the man and put him in the garden of Eden to work it and keep it."

Now out of the ground the LORD God had formed every beast of the field and every bird of the heavens and brought them to the man to see what he would call them. And whatever the man called every living creature, that was its name. (Genesis 2:15, 19)

5   Where it was put into practice, this vision of work made the system of slavery in the Roman Empire more humane. Its full implementation with all of its implications, with the biblical teaching on the *imago Dei* and the universality of God's redemptive love in Christ, entails the abolition of slavery. A persecuted minority, early Christians were not in a position to abolish slavery in the empire; nevertheless, they carried the seeds of abolition with them.

6   See:

For it will be like a man going on a journey, who called his servants and entrusted to them his property. To one he gave five talents, to another two, to another one, to each according to his ability. Then he went away. He who had received the five talents went at once and traded with them, and he made five talents more. So also he who had the two talents made two talents more. But he who had received the one talent went and dug in the ground and hid his master's money. Now after a long time the master of those servants came and settled accounts with them. And he who had received the five talents came forward, bringing five talents more, saying, 'Master, you delivered to me five talents; here I have made five talents more.' His master said to him, 'Well done, good and faithful servant. You have been faithful over a little; I will set you over much. Enter into the joy of your master.' And he also who had the two talents came forward, saying, 'Master, you delivered to me two talents; here I have made two talents more.' His master said to him, 'Well done, good and faithful servant. You have been faithful over a little; I will set you over much. Enter into the joy of your master.' He also who had received the one talent came forward, saying, 'Master, I knew you to be a hard man, reaping where you did not sow, and gathering where you scattered no seed, so I was afraid, and I went and hid your talent in the ground. Here you have what is yours.' But his master answered him, 'You wicked and slothful servant! You knew that I reap where I have not sown and gather where I scattered no seed? Then you ought to have invested my money with the bankers, and at my coming I should have received what was my own with interest. So take the talent from him and give it to him who has the ten talents. For to everyone who has will more be given, and he will have an abundance. But from the one who has not, even what he has will be taken away. And cast the worthless servant into the outer darkness. In that place there will be weeping and gnashing of teeth. (Matthew 25:14-30)

7   Alan Richardson wrote: "The biblical writers do not consider that work is degrading. Unlike the Greeks, who thought that working for one's living was beneath the dignity of a gentleman, the Hebrews looked upon daily work as a normal part of the divine ordering of the world." Alan Richardson, *The Biblical Doctrine of Work* (London: SCM Press LTD, p. 20.

8   Manual labor, especially, was regarded as work fit only for slaves (which were abundant in both Greek and Roman societies). In classical Greek the word for work is *ponos*, which has the same root as the Latin *poena*, meaning *sorrow*. See Colin Brown, ed., *The New International Dictionary of New Testament Theology* (Grand Rapids: Zondervan Publishing House, 1981), Vol. I, p. 62.

9   Henry Van Til wrote: "All of man's activity under the sun, therefore, is not for himself, but unto the Lord: work and play, eating and drinking, buying and selling, begetting

children and giving them in marriage, building houses and living in them." Henry R. Van Til, *The Calvinistic Concept of Culture* (Grand Rapids, MI: Baker Book House Company, 1972), p. 195.

10   This will give you some sense of the original meaning of these words:

> The modern ecclesiastical use of the word liturgy is quite different from the original meaning of [*leitourgeo, leitourgia*] which were wholly secular terms. . . . . [*Leitourgeo*] is the direct discharge of specific services to the body politic. . . . . the technical political useage extended to cover all kinds of services to the body politic . . . . From the technical and wider use there then develops a general and non-technical use . . . . Aristotle uses [*leitourgein*] e.g., for the private services of slaves to their masters or of workers to their taskmasters.

Gerhard Kittel, ed., *Theological Dictionary of the New Testament*, trans. and ed., Geoffrey W. Bromiley (Grand Rapids, MI: Wm. B. Eerdmans Publishing Company, 1967), Vol. IV, pp. 215-17.

11   Or the cognate verb *leitergeo*.

12   As C.S. Lewis put it, "The work of a Beethoven, and the work of a charwoman, become spiritual on precisely the same condition, that of being offered to God, of being done humbly 'as to the Lord.'" C.S. Lewis, "Learning in War-Time" in *Weight of Glory*, p. 55.

13   See:

> The earth is the LORD's and the fullness thereof,
>   the world and those who dwell therein. (Psalm 24:1)

> For every beast of the forest is mine,
>   the cattle on a thousand hills.
> I know all the birds of the hills,
>   and all that moves in the field is mine. (Psalm 51:10-11)

14   Luther observed that God "gives the wool, but not without our labor. If it is on the sheep, it makes no garment." Quoted in Gustaf Wingren, *Luther on Vocation*, trans. Carl C. Rasmussen (Philadelphia: Muhlenburg Press, 1957), p. 8.

15   Work and worship are united in the Eucharist. Alan Richardson wrote:

> Surely there must be some significance in the fact that the sacramental elements in the Eucharist . . . are manufactured articles: it was these artefacts of human labour that Jesus in the upper room took and blessed and gave. Moreover, before God's sacramental gift of the Body and the Blood of Christ can be received by the faithful, bread and wine, products of human labour, must be laid upon the altar or table – call it what we will – whether they are placed there solemnly, liturgically, in the offertory, or whether they are put there unceremoniously by the vestry-clerk before the service begins. Without the offering of human hands there will be no sacrament. But equally, without the toil and skill of the farmer, without the labour of the bakers, the transport workers, the banks and offices, the shops and distributors – without, in fact, the toil of

mines and shipyards and steel-works and so on – this loaf would not have been here to lay upon the altar this morning. In truth, the whole world of human work is involved in the manufacture of the bread and wine which we offer in the Eucharist, and which is given back to us as God's ineffable gift. Here is enshrined the whole mystery of man's labour as well as the whole drama of man's redemption. Here is the perfect symbol of the unity of work and worship, the strange unbreakable link that exists between the bread that is won in the sweat of man's face and the bread of life that is bought without money and without price.

Alan Richardson, *The Biblical Doctrine of Work*, pp. 67-68.

[16] Abraham Kuyper, *Abraham Kuyper: A Centennial Reader*, ed. James D. Bratt (Grand Rapids, Mich.: Eerdmans, 1998), p. 488.

[17] C.S. Lewis wrote:

It is not so much of our time and so much of our attention that God demands; it is not even all our time and all our attention; it is ourselves. . . . For some (nobody knows which) the Christian life will include much leisure, many occupations we naturally like. But these will be received from God's hands. In a perfect Christian they would be as much part of his "religion," his "service," as his hardest duties, and his feasts would be as Christian as his fasts. What cannot be admitted – what must exist only as an undefeated but daily resisted enemy – is the idea of something that is "our own," some area in which we are to be "out of school," on which God has no claim.

C.S. Lewis, "A Slip of the Tongue," in The Weight of Glory: *And Other Addresses* (New York, NY: HaperCollins, 1980) p. 189.

[18] Robert N. Bellah, "Is There a Common American Culture?" found at: http://www.robertbellah.com/articles_6.htm.

[19] Robert N. Bellah, Richard Madsen, William M. Sullivan, Ann Swidler, and Steven M. Tipton, *Habits of the Heart: Individualism and Commitment in American Life* (New York: Harper & Row, 1986), pp. 287-88.

[20] I understand the polemic between Luther and the Roman Catholic church over the role of works in salvation and take my stand with him in that regard. I differ with him, however, in his belief that good works are directed toward our neighbors, as an expression of love for them, but not toward God. See Gustaf Wingren, *Luther on Vocation*, trans. Carl C. Rasmussen (Philadelphia: Muhlenberg Press, 1957), p. 10. They are not a means of reaching toward God for salvation; they are offered to God for his glory in the world, and, as such, are an expression of our love for him.

[21] Matthew 5:16

[22] Gustaf Wingren, *Luther on Vocation*, p. 43.

[23] Ibid., p. 45.

24   Ibid., p. 47.

25   Donald Bloesch writes, "The evangelical Christian does not believe that one can merit salvation by good works but that good works will flow spontaneously out of a joyful heart." Donald G. Bloesch, *Freedom for Obedience: Evangelical Ethics in Contemporary Times* (San Francisco: Harper and Row, 1987), p. 32.

26   To turn a phrase used by C.S. Lewis. C.S. Lewis, *Mere Christianity* (New York: Simon & Schuster. Touchstone Edition, 1996), p. 153.

27   Ephesians 4:28

28   Karl Barth, *Church Dogmatics*, eds., G.W. Bromiley, T.F. Torrance (London, New York: T & T Clark International, 2004), Vol. 3.4, p. 381.

CHAPTER 4 JOY AT WORK: REDEMPTION, PART 2

1   This is the larger passage, of which this quote is a part:

> Though we are creatures who share in the fate of other creatures – we are born, experience suffering and joy, and will die – our existence is elevated by our unique calling and responsibility to highlight and promote the presence of God within creation and to enable creatures to share in the praise of their Maker. . . . Our entire life, and thus also our work, must be understood and carried out in orientation and conversation with God.

Norman Wirzba, *Living the Sabbath: Discovering the Rhythms of Rest and Delight,* (Grand Rapids, Michigan: Brazos Press, 2006), p. 96.

2   The preposition denotes accompaniment or association. It can also be translated *with*.

3   1 Corinthians 3:9

4   2 Corinthians 1:24. See also:

> . . . and so do Mark, Aristarchus, Demas, and Luke, my fellow workers. (Philemon 1:24)

> Therefore we ought to support people like these, that we may be fellow workers for the truth. (3 John 1:8)

5   Paul put this important notion of collaboration into the context of the Kingdom of God:

> Aristarchus my fellow prisoner greets you, and Mark the cousin of Barnabas (concerning whom you have received instructions—if he comes to you, welcome him), and Jesus who is called Justus. These are the only men of the circumcision among my fellow workers (*synergoi*) for the kingdom of God, and they have been a comfort to me. (Colossians 4:11)

It would never have occurred to Paul (or to any first century follower of Jesus) to put the Kingdom into an isolated category of personal salvation. The Kingdom is all-encompassing. It embraces every facet of life. It is the remaking of the world in harmony with the will of God. We work together for the Kingdom, and when the Kingdom is manifested in our work, it becomes joyful collaboration.

6 "But you are a chosen race, a royal priesthood, a holy nation, a people for his own possession, that you may proclaim the excellencies of him who called you out of darkness into his marvelous light." (1 Peter 2:9)

7 There is a very great irony here. In medieval Europe vocation was an exalted term, reserved for clergy. In our day – at least in educational settings – it has become a demeaning term, applied to a lower class of workers. What is true on both sides of the irony is that it is used to divide people and work in unhealthy ways.

8 Martin Luther, in *Luther's Works*, ed. Helmut T. Lehmann (Philadelphia: Muhlenberg Press, 1962), Vol. 5, p. 102.

9 Martin Luther, *Luther's Works*, Vol. 46, p. 246.

10 Martin Luther, *Luther's Works*, Vol. 2, p. 349.

11 Martin Luther, in *Luther's Works*, Vol. 46, p. 241

12 Ibid., p. 253

13 John Calvin, *Institutes of the Christian Religion*, trans. Henry Beveridge (Grand Rapids: Willliam B. Eerdmans Publishing Co., eighth print., 1979), Vol. II, p. 34.

Alister McGrath has written of Calvin:

> Calvin also articulated a work ethic that strongly encouraged the development of Geneva's enterprise culture. He taught that the individual believer has a vocation to serve God in the world—in every sphere of human existence—lending a new dignity and meaning to ordinary work. Calvin agreed that the world should be treated with contempt to the extent that it is not God, and is too easily mistaken for Him; yet, it is the creation of God, to be affirmed at least to a degree. "Let believers get used to a contempt of the present life that gives rise to no hatred of it, or ingratitude towards God. . . . Something that is neither blessed nor desirable in itself can become something good for the devout." Christians are thus to inhabit the world with joy and gratitude, without becoming trapped within it. A degree of critical detachment must accompany Christian affirmation of the world as God's creation and gift. Christians are to live in the world, while avoiding falling into that world, becoming immersed within and swallowed by it.

Alister McGrath, "Calvin and the Christian Calling" in *First Things*, (June/July 1999), pp. 31-35, published online at http://www.firstthings.com/article/1999/06/calvin-and-the-christian-calling.

[14]   Christopher Lasch explores the impact of the loss of Protestant work ethic and its virtues, and the emergence of self-preservation as the new guiding principle in the American work place. See *The Culture of Narcissism: American Life in An Age of Diminishing Expectations* (New York, NY: W.W. Horton and Company, 1979), pp. 52-70.

Robert Bellah and his colleagues explore the same theme. See Robert N. Bellah, Richard Madsen, William M. Sullivan, Ann Swidler, and Steven M. Tipton, *Habits of the Heart: Individualism and Commitment in American Life* (New York: Harper & Row, 1986

[15]   Romans 15:18

[16]   "For from him and through him and to him are all things. To him be glory forever. Amen." (Romans 11:36)

[17]   Quoted in Gene Edward Veith, "Our Calling and God's Glory" at: http://www.modernreformation.org/default.php?page=articledisplay&var1=ArtRead&var2=881.

[18]   Paul was called to be an apostle, but he was not paid to be one. His opportunities for employment were in his trade as a tent-maker.

[19]   Your special calling in life will likely involve the stewardship of natural and spiritual gifts that are uniquely yours. God may call us in other ways, as well, but he does not give us gifts for nothing! The apostle Paul wrote: "For we are his workmanship, created in Christ Jesus for good works, which God prepared beforehand, that we should walk in them." (Ephesians 2:10) The good works that God has designed for us (another way of talking about our special calling) are related to his handiwork in our lives.

[20]   This is what the Westminster Divines called "The chief end of man." *The Confession of Faith of The Presbyterian Church in the United States* (Atlanta: John Knox Press, 1965), p. 287.

[21]   1 Corinthians 1:9

[22]   "We exhorted each one of you and encouraged you and charged you to walk in a manner worthy of God, who calls you into his own kingdom and glory." (1 Thessalonians 2:12)

[23]   Colossians 3:17

[24]   Paul characteristically began his letters by referring to his call to be an apostle. See these examples:

Paul, a servant of Christ Jesus, called to be an apostle. (Romans 1:1)

Paul, called by the will of God to be an apostle of Christ Jesus. (1 Corinthians 1:1)

Paul, an apostle of Christ Jesus by the will of God. (2 Corinthians 1:1)

25 "But seek first the kingdom of God and his righteousness, and all these things will be added to you." (Matthew 6:33)

26 See, for instance, the last chapter of Rick Howe, *Path of Life: Finding the Joy You've Always Longed For* (Boulder, CO: University Ministries Press, 2017).and the last four chapters of Rick Howe, *River of Delights: Quenching Your Thirst For Joy* (Boulder, CO: University Ministries Press, 2017).

27 Dallas Willard, *The Divine Conspiracy: Rediscovering Our Hidden Life in God* (San Francisco: CA: HarperSanFrancisco, 1998), p. 26.

28 Os Guinness, *The Call: Finding and Fulfilling the Central Purpose of Your Life* (Nashville: Thomas Nelson, 2003), p. 29.

29 "God is faithful, by whom you were called into the fellowship of his Son, Jesus Christ our Lord." (1 Corinthians 1:9)

30 "We exhorted each one of you and encouraged you and charged you to walk in a manner worthy of God, who calls you into his own kingdom and glory." (1 Thessalonians 2:12)

31 "But as he who called you is holy, you also be holy in all your conduct." (1 Peter 1:15)

32 See:

> Bondservants, obey in everything those who are your earthly masters, not by way of eye-service, as people-pleasers, but with sincerity of heart, fearing the Lord. Whatever you do, work heartily, as for the Lord and not for men, knowing that from the Lord you will receive the inheritance as your reward. You are serving the Lord Christ. (Colossians 3:22-24)

33 See Jesus' Parable of the Talents in Matthew 25:14-30.

34 See:

> "Teacher, which is the great commandment in the Law?" And he said to him, "You shall love the Lord your God with all your heart and with all your soul and with all your mind. This is the great and first commandment. And a second is like it: You shall love your neighbor as yourself. On these two commandments depend all the Law and the Prophets." (Matthew 22:36-40)

35 Ephesians 2:10

36 Frederick Buechner, *Wishful Thinking: A Theological ABC* (San Francisco: HarperSanFrancisco, 1993), p. 119.

37 "But as for me, my prayer is to you, O LORD.

At an acceptable time, O God,
in the abundance of your steadfast love
answer me in your saving faithfulness." (Psalm 69:13)

³⁸ James 1:5

³⁹ James 1:6-8

⁴⁰ Mark 9:24

⁴¹ See the following:

> Truly, I say to you, if you have faith like a grain of mustard seed, you will say to this mountain, 'Move from here to there,' and it will move, and nothing will be impossible for you. (Matthew 17:20)

> As they passed by in the morning, they saw the fig tree withered away to its roots. And Peter remembered and said to him, 'Rabbi, look! The fig tree that you cursed has withered.' And Jesus answered them, "Have faith in God. Truly, I say to you, whoever says to this mountain, 'Be taken up and thrown into the sea,' and does not doubt in his heart, but believes that what he says will come to pass, it will be done for him. Therefore I tell you, whatever you ask in prayer, believe that you have received it, and it will be yours. And whenever you stand praying, forgive, if you have anything against anyone, so that your Father also who is in heaven may forgive you your trespasses. (Mark 11:20-26)

CHAPTER 5 JOY AT REST: SABBATH, PART 1

¹ See:

> Have you not known? Have you not heard?
> The LORD is the everlasting God,
> the Creator of the ends of the earth.
> He does not faint or grow weary;
> his understanding is unsearchable. (Isaiah 40:28)

² Genesis 1:31. The Hebrew word that describes God's appraisal of his handiwork (*tov*) means "pleasant, agreeable, good," when it is used of things, or "glad or happy" when it is used of people. Note the emphasis: very good!

³ See its title: "A Song for the Sabbath."

⁴ See:

> "If you turn back your foot from the Sabbath,
> from doing your pleasure on my holy day,
> and call the Sabbath a delight
> and the holy day of the LORD honorable;

if you honor it, not going your own ways,
    or seeking your own pleasure, or talking idly." (Isaiah 58:13)

5   The Sabbath was not given to individuals, but to a nation. It is a corporate command. It is meant to be shared.

6   J.I. Packer summarizes the Puritan view of the Christian Sabbath, including the characteristic theme of joy:

> Sabbath-keeping is not a tedious burden, but a joyful privilege. The Sabbath is not a fast, but a feast, a day for rejoicing in the works of a gracious God, and joy must be its temper throughout (cf. Is 58:3). Joy suits no person so much as a saint, and it becomes no season as well as a sabbath.

> It is the duty and glory of a Christian to rejoice in the Lord every day, but especially on the Lord's Day. . . . To fast on the Lord's Day, saith Ignatius, is to kill Christ; but to rejoice in the Lord this day, and to rejoice in all the duties of the day . . . this is to crown Christ, this is to lift up Christ.

> Joy must be the keynote of public worship. Baxter in particular deplores drab, mournful services. There must be no gloom on the Lord's Day. And those who say that they cannot find joy in the spiritual exercises of a Christian Sunday thereby show that there is something very wrong with them.

J.I. Packer, *A Quest for Godliness: The Puritan Vision of the Christian Life* (Wheaton, IL: Crossway Books: 1990), p. 239.

7   I am inclined to believe that the Exodus commandment makes explicit what was already implicit in Genesis 2:3, with the words "God blessed the seventh day and made it holy." If this is so, the sacred pattern given as a "creation ordinance" pre-dates the Exodus, was interrupted by Israel's captivity in Egypt and the oppressive demands of slavery, and was then re-instituted at Sinai. The "remembering" pointed them back to an earlier time when they enjoyed a healthier pattern of life.

8   There are no sacred and secular categories of life before God. All of life is sacred before him. Our only options are to celebrate what is sacred or to profane or desecrate it.

9   Mark 2:27. The Greek word for "man" here is *anthropos* (the generic term for human beings), which is consistent with seeing the Sabbath command (as it was first given) as a creation ordinance, and not something specific to Israel.

10   Psalm 127:2

11   Latin for "for the perpetual remembrance of the thing."

12   See the following:

> For six years you shall sow your land and gather in its yield, but the seventh year you shall let it rest and lie fallow, that the poor of your people may eat; and what they leave the beasts of the field may eat. You shall do likewise with your vineyard, and with your olive orchard. (Exodus 23:10-11)

The LORD spoke to Moses on Mount Sinai, saying, "Speak to the people of Israel and say to them, When you come into the land that I give you, the land shall keep a Sabbath to the LORD. For six years you shall sow your field, and for six years you shall prune your vineyard and gather in its fruits, but in the seventh year there shall be a Sabbath of solemn rest for the land, a Sabbath to the LORD. You shall not sow your field or prune your vineyard. You shall not reap what grows of itself in your harvest, or gather the grapes of your undressed vine. It shall be a year of solemn rest for the land. The Sabbath of the land shall provide food for you, for yourself and for your male and female slaves and for your hired worker and the sojourner who lives with you, and for your cattle and for the wild animals that are in your land: all its yield shall be for food." (Leviticus 25: 1-7)

[13]   See:

You shall count seven weeks of years, seven times seven years, so that the time of the seven weeks of years shall give you forty-nine years. Then you shall sound the loud trumpet on the tenth day of the seventh month. On the Day of Atonement you shall sound the trumpet throughout all your land. And you shall consecrate the fiftieth year, and proclaim liberty throughout the land to all its inhabitants. It shall be a jubilee for you, when each of you shall return to his property and each of you shall return to his clan. That fiftieth year shall be a jubilee for you; in it you shall neither sow nor reap what grows of itself nor gather the grapes from the undressed vines. For it is a jubilee. It shall be holy to you. You may eat the produce of the field. In this year of jubilee each of you shall return to his property. And if you make a sale to your neighbor or buy from your neighbor, you shall not wrong one another. You shall pay your neighbor according to the number of years after the jubilee, and he shall sell to you according to the number of years for crops. If the years are many, you shall increase the price, and if the years are few, you shall reduce the price, for it is the number of the crops that he is selling to you. You shall not wrong one another, but you shall fear your God, for I am the LORD your God. (Leviticus 25:8-17)

[14]   The *agape* feast was celebrated by the early Church likely until it was banned by the Romans as the meal of a secret society. Our celebration of the Lord's Supper, or Eucharist, has lost its original context of communal meal. This is seen clearly in the Last Supper: "Now as they were eating [the Passover meal], Jesus took bread, and after blessing it broke it and gave it to the disciples, and said, "Take, eat; this is my body." (Matthew 26:26)

It is also seen in Paul's instructions to the church at Corinth:

When you come together, it is not the Lord's supper that you eat. For in eating, each one goes ahead with his own meal. One goes hungry, another gets drunk. What! Do you not have houses to eat and drink in? Or do you despise the church of God and humiliate those who have nothing? What shall I say to you? Shall I commend you in this? No, I will not. For I received from the Lord what I also delivered to you, that the Lord Jesus on the night when he was betrayed took bread, and when he had given thanks, he broke it, and said, "This is my body which is for you. Do this in remembrance of me." In the same way also he took the cup, after supper, saying, "This cup is the new covenant in my blood. Do this, as often as you drink it, in remembrance of me." For as often as you eat this bread and drink the cup, you proclaim the Lord's death until he comes. (1 Corinthians 11:20-26)

According to the *International Standard Bible Encyclopedia*:

114

In the opinion of the great majority of scholars, the Agape as a meal at which not only bread and wine, but all kinds of viands were used, a meal which had the double purpose of satisfying hunger and thirst and giving expression to the sense of Christian brotherhood.. At the end of this feast, bread and wine were taken according to the Lord's command, and after thanksgiving to God were eaten and drunk in remembrance of Christ, and as a special means of communion with the Lord Himself and through Him with one another.

Found at: http://.internationalstandardbible.com/A/agape.html.

[15] Alexander Roberts, James Donaldson, eds., *Ante-Nicene Fathers* (Peabody, MA: Hendrickson Publishers, Inc., 1994), Vol. 3, p. 47.

[16] Ibid., p. 46.

CHAPTER 6 JOY AT REST: SABBATH, PART 2

[1]   See:

> Your new moons and your appointed feasts
>   my soul hates;
> they have become a burden to me,
>   I am weary of bearing them.
> When you spread forth your hands,
>   I will hide my eyes from you;
> even though you make many prayers,
>   I will not listen;
>   your hands are full of blood.
> Wash yourselves; make yourselves clean;
>   remove the evil of your doings
>   from before my eyes;
> cease to do evil,
>   learn to do good;
> seek justice,
>   correct oppression;
> defend the fatherless,
>   plead for the widow. (Isaiah 1:14-17)

[2]   It is possible that the fourth commandment in the Mosaic legislation referred to a practice already ancient and well known from the patriarchal period, but that had been interrupted by Israel's captivity in Egypt and its work week and work regulations for the Jews.

Even if that was not the case, my point stands. When the law was given by Moses, Israel was still hundreds of years away from the united monarchy under Solomon, when the temple became part of the nation's worship.

[3]   The first temple dates to the reign of Solomon (ca. 961-922 B.C.)

4   The synagogue system arose in the post-exilic period, after 539 B.C.

5   As we saw in the last chapter, the Sabbath tradition in the Torah developed over time. Its significance was not given all at once at the beginning.

6   There are many ways in which a local church might include ministries of compassion in its weekly assemblies. These suggestions focus on economic need, but many other expressions of compassion are possible:

> ➢ Offer a breakfast or lunch for the needy before or after a worship service.

> ➢ Offer food baskets and grocery store gift cards, and announce this opportunity from the pulpit.

> ➢ Invite the poor and homeless home for a meal after a worship service.

> ➢ Create a congregational employment network, and a staffed table to facilitate connections.

> ➢ Provide information that will facilitate the church's involvement in ministries of compassion in the community.

7   Luke 4:16. Some of my messianic Jewish friends see this creating an obligation for all Christ-followers. As a matter of general hermeneutics, it is questionable methodology to make actions in a historical narrative a transcendent norm. Because Jesus walked through grainfields on the Sabbath (Matthew 12:1), must we? There is a more specific question of interpretation, however, concerning the words "And as was his custom, he went to the synagogue on the Sabbath day, and he stood up to read." D.A. Carson comments:

> But what is the nature of the custom of Jesus to which Luke refers? Is it synagogue attendance per se; hence raising the possibility in some minds that Jesus is set before Luke's readers as a model of reverence for the Sabbath? Or is it Jesus' more recently acquired habit of teaching in the synagogues that is primarily in view (c.f. the preceding verse!)? The latter alternative is almost certainly to be preferred. . . . The mention of Jesus and Paul [Acts 17:2] as constantly in the synagogues . . . therefore primarily reflects the opportunities presented to them to teach; it provides little real evidence of theological commitment on behalf of Jesus or Paul to Sabbath worship (even less, of course, to Sunday worship).

D.A. Carson, "The Sabbath, Sunday, and the Law in Luke/Acts" in D.A. Carson, ed. *From Sabbath to Lord's Day: A Biblical, Historical and Theological Investigation* (Grand Rapids, Michigan: The Zondervan Corporation, 1982), pp. 101-102.

8   Norman Wirzba, *Living the Sabbath: Discovering the Rhythms of Rest and Delight* (Grand Rapids, Michigan: Brazos Press, 2006), p. 43.

9   "So the Son of Man is lord even of the Sabbath." (Mark 2:28)

¹⁰ "Do not think that I have come to abolish the Law or the Prophets; I have not come to abolish them but to fulfill them." (Matthew 5:17)

¹¹ "And likewise the cup after they had eaten, saying, 'This cup that is poured out for you is the new covenant in my blood.'" (Luke 22:20)
Jesus' reference to a new covenant hearkens back to the prophecy of Jeremiah:

> "Behold, the days are coming, declares the LORD, when I will make a new covenant with the house of Israel and the house of Judah, not like the covenant that I made with their fathers on the day when I took them by the hand to bring them out of the land of Egypt, my covenant that they broke, though I was their husband, declares the LORD. For this is the covenant that I will make with the house of Israel after those days, declares the LORD: I will put my law within them, and I will write it on their hearts. And I will be their God, and they shall be my people. And no longer shall each one teach his neighbor and each his brother, saying, 'Know the LORD,' for they shall all know me, from the least of them to the greatest, declares the LORD. For I will forgive their iniquity, and I will remember their sin no more." (Jeremiah 31:31-34)

¹² Matthew 11:28

¹³ I respectfully acknowledge my Seventh Day Adventist and Messianic Jewish friends who disagree with me on this issue. It is not my intent to drive a wedge in relationships between any who follow Christ. I understand their arguments; they are just not persuasive to me (nor mine to them!). We disagree on Sabbath and calendar, but we agree on the Lordship of Christ and his worthiness to be worshiped seven days a week.

The days of the week, including the day we set apart for rest and for worship, are shadows. Christ is the blazing sun: "Therefore let no one pass judgment on you in questions of food and drink, or with regard to a festival or a new moon or a Sabbath. These are a shadow of the things to come, but the substance belongs to Christ." (Colossians 2:16-17)

¹⁴ For a thorough study of the Sabbath and the Lord's Day, see Carson, *From Sabbath to Lord's Day.*

¹⁵ Some Christians hold the position that the Sabbath has been done away with, and that the Christian celebration of the Lord's Day stands entirely on its own. This is based largely on a view that the Sabbath was part of Israel's ceremonial law – which has been abrogated with the inauguration of the new covenant. The Sabbath is far more than that, however. It is grounded originally in creation, not in priesthood and ceremonial regulations.

¹⁶ 2 Corinthians 5:17

¹⁷ Luke 22:19

¹⁸ Paul's teaching captures the past and future dimensions of the Lord's Supper: "For as often as you eat this bread and drink the cup, you proclaim the Lord's death [in history] until he comes [in the future]. (1 Corinthians 11:26)

19 See also:

> . . . waiting for and hastening the coming of the day of God, because of which the heavens will be set on fire and dissolved, and the heavenly bodies will melt as they burn! But according to his promise we are waiting for new heavens and a new earth in which righteousness dwells. (2 Peter 3:12-13)

> Then I saw a new heaven and a new earth, for the first heaven and the first earth had passed away, and the sea was no more. (Revelation 21:1)

20 Norman Wirzba writes:

> Though Sunday is the first day of the week, in terms of the seven-day creation of the world it also stands beyond creation as its final summation or conclusion. We should, therefore, think of Sunday as an intensification of the Sabbath, a new beginning for creation, because it represents the "age to come." It is an eschatological reality, which means that on this day Jesus has opened up new possibilities for genuine life. Possibilities that have been set in motion but are not yet fully complete.

Wirzba, *Living the Sabbath*, p. 49.

21 This future rest is the rest of the Sabbath promised in the Book of Hebrews: "So then, there remains a Sabbath rest for the people of God, for whoever has entered God's rest has also rested from his works as God did from his. Let us therefore strive to enter that rest." (Hebrews 4: 9-11) Having completed our work on earth as his stewards, we will hear the words of the risen Christ: "Well done, good and faithful servant. You have been faithful over a little; I will set you over much. Enter into the joy of your master." (Matthew 25:21)

CHAPTER 7 JOY AT PLAY, PART 1

1 Josef Pieper, *Leisure: The Basis of Culture*, trans., Gerald Malsbary (South Bend, Indiana: St. Augustine Press, Inc., 1998), pp. 54-55.

2 Lewis Smedes, "Theology and the Playful Life," in *God and the Good: Essays in Honor of Henry Stob*, eds., Clifton Orlebeke and Lewis Smedes (Grand Rapids, MI: William B. Eerdmans Publishing Co., 1975), pp. 55-56. Emphasis added.

3 "God created the world not out of reason or necessity or practicality, but out of sheer joy. It is all gloriously superfluous." Peter Kreeft, *Heaven: The Heart's Deepest Longing* (San Francisco: Ignatius Press, 1989), p. 144.

4 Smedes, *God and the Good*, p. 56.

5 Jürgen Moltmann, *Theology of Play*, trans. Reinhard Ulrich (U.S.A.: Harper & Row, Publishers, 1972), p.17.

6   It is translated as laugh, play, merry-making, playing instrumental music, singing and dancing. *A Hebrew and English Lexicon of the Old Testament*, eds., Francis Brown, S.R. Driver, and Charles A. Briggs (Oxford: Clarendon Press, Reprint. 1953), pp. 965-66.

7   "And David returned to bless his household. But Michal the daughter of Saul came out to meet David and said, 'How the king of Israel honored himself today, uncovering himself today before the eyes of his servants' female servants, as one of the vulgar fellows shamelessly uncovers himself!'" (2 Samuel 6:20)

8   See the following:

    And when he had removed him, he raised up David to be their king; of whom he testified and said, 'I have found in David the son of Jesse a man after my heart, who will do all my will.' (Acts 13:22)

    And Samuel said to Saul, "You have done foolishly; you have not kept the commandment of the LORD your God, which he commanded you; for now the LORD would have established your kingdom over Israel for ever. But now your kingdom shall not continue; the LORD has sought out a man after his own heart; and the LORD has appointed him to be prince over his people, because you have not kept what the LORD commanded you." (1 Samuel 13:13-14)

9   One of the names given to our species, in fact, is *homo ludens*, or man the player.

10 See the following:

    [Jesus] said, "Truly, I say to you, unless you turn and become like children, you will never enter the kingdom of heaven. Whoever humbles himself like this child is the greatest in the kingdom of heaven." (Matthew 18:3-4)

    Jesus said, "Let the little children come to me and do not hinder them, for to such belongs the kingdom of heaven." (Matthew 19:14)

11 "And the streets of the city will be filled with boys and girls playing in its streets." (Zechariah 8:5)

12 Malachi 4:2

13 See Derek Kidner, *A Commentary on Books III and IV of the Psalms* (London: Inter-Varsity Press, 1975), p.372, and C.F. Keil and F. Delitzsch, Commentary on the Old Testament in Ten Volumes, trans. James Martin (Grand Rapids, MI: Eerdmans Publishing Company, 1984), Vol. III, p. 135.

14 Robert K. Johnston, *The Christian at Play* (Grand Rapids: Eerdmans Publishing Company, 1983), pp. 123-124.

15 John Calvin, *Sermons on Deuteronomy*, trans. Arthur Golding (Philadelphia: The Banner of Truth Trust, 1987), p. 204. This is a modern rendering of the original 16th century translation.

Question 60 of The Westminster Shorter Catechism asks how we should observe the Sabbath and then answers: "The Sabbath is to be sanctified by a holy resting all that day, even from such worldly employments and recreations as are lawful on other days; and spending the whole time in the public and private exercises of God's worship, except so much as is to be taken up in the works of necessity and mercy." *The Confession of Faith of The Presbyterian Church in the United States* (Atlanta: John Knox Press, 1965), p. 307.

[16] Robert K. Johnston, *The Christian at Play*, p. 93. Emphasis added.

[17] Before the face of God.

[18] See "Calvin in the Hands of the Philistines: Or Did Calvin Bowl on the Sabbath?"
at
http://www.naphtali.com/articles/chris-coldwell/calvin-in-the-hands-of-the-philistines-or-did-calvin-bowl-on-the-sabbath/

See also R.C. Sproul's article, "Defining the Debate" at www.ligonier.org/learn/articles/defining-debate.

[19] Henry R. Van Til, *The Calvinistic Concept of Culture* (Grand Rapids, MI: Baker Book House Company, 1972), p. 93.

CHAPTER 8 JOY AT PLAY, PART 2

[1] C.S. Lewis, "Christianity and Culture" in *Christian Reflections*, ed. Walter Hooper (Grand Rapids, MI: Eerdmans, 1995), pp. 33-34.

[2] This understanding of joy lies buried in the etymology of the word in our own language. Our English word "joy" comes from the Latin *gaudium*, which was used not only of joy, delight, and gladness, but of "physical or sensual delight." See *The Oxford Latin Dictionary*, ed., P.G.W. Glare (Oxford: The Clarendon Press, 1982), p. 755.

[3] Rick Howe, *Path of Life: Finding the Joy You've Always Longed For* (Boulder, CO: University Ministries Press, 2017), p. 2.

[4] Nicholas Wolterstorff, *Art in Action: Toward a Christian Aesthetic* (Grand Rapids, MI: William B. Eerdmans Publishing Co., 1980), p. 79. P. Daniel Maguire says that the biblical concept of shalom, or peace, "for the Hebrews was the fulfillment of our capacity for rejoicing." Daniel C. Maguire, *The Moral Core of Judaism and Christianity: Reclaiming the Revolution* (Minneapolis: Fortress Press, 1993), p. 236.

[5] Quoted in Moltmann, *Theology of Play*, pp. 36-37.

[6] Watching professional sports may be entertainment (and even part of our rest), but it is not play, and should never be a substitute for play. There are no couch potatoes in heaven!

7   I don't say this to demean professional sports, or to deny that many professional athletes love their sport and find great pleasure in it, but to see professionalism in its proper perspective. It is work, and should be treated as such. It is neither greater nor less than any other labor.

8   Our word *amateur* comes from the Italian *amatore*, which, in turn, came from the Latin *amator* 'lover,' and *amare* 'to love.'

9   On the persecution of the Jews under Antiochus and the Seleucids, historian John Bright wrote:

> A gymnasium was established in Jerusalem and young men enrolled in it; all sorts of Greek sports were fostered, as were Greek fashions of dress. Young priests neglected their duties to compete in the games. Embarrassed by their circumcision, since sports were participated in naked (cf. Jub. 3:31), many Jews submitted to surgery to disguise it. Conservative Jews, profoundly shocked, regarded all this as outright apostasy. Nor were they wrong. The gymnasium was not a mere sporting club, nor did its opponents object merely to what they considered immodest and indecent behavior. The status of Jewish religion was in question. The gymnasium seems actually to have been a separate corporation of Hellenized Jews, with definite legal and civic rights, set up within the city of Jerusalem. Since Greek sports were inseparable from the cult of Heracles (II Macc. 4:18-20), or of Hermes, or of the royal house, membership in the gymnasium inevitably involved some degree of recognition of the gods who were its protectors.

John Bright, *A History of Israel*, fourth edition (Louisville, KY: Westminster John Knox Press, 2000), p. 420.

10   See also:

> For this I toil, struggling with all his energy that he powerfully works within me. (Colossians 1:29)

> Fight the good fight of the faith. Take hold of the eternal life to which you were called and about which you made the good confession in the presence of many witnesses. (1 Timothy 6:12)

> Therefore, since we are surrounded by so great a cloud of witnesses, let us also lay aside every weight, and sin which clings so closely, and let us run with endurance the race that is set before us. (Hebrews 12:1)

> Beloved, although I was very eager to write to you about our common salvation, I found it necessary to write appealing to you to contend for the faith that was once for all delivered to the saints. (Jude 1:3)

11   Wolterstorff, *Art in Action*, p. 68. He applies this truth to art.

12   This is true even if the venue for play moves indoors, and if the celebration of the goodness of God's creation becomes more focused on our sisters and brothers in creation, food and refreshment, and games at a dining room table or in a living room.

13   The word enthusiast is a theological term. It comes from the Greek *enthousiastēs*: one who is inspired by a god.

14   In Luke 11:11-13 Jesus says, "What father among you, if his son asks for a fish, will instead of a fish give him a serpent; or if he asks for an egg, will give him a scorpion? If you then, who are evil, know how to give good gifts to your children, how much more will the heavenly Father give the Holy Spirit to those who ask him!"

15   "Every good endowment and every perfect gift is from above, coming down from the Father of lights with whom there is no variation or shadow due to change." (James 1:17)

16   Proverbs 27:17

17   Or moral virtue in an athletic setting.

18   Howe, *Path of Life*, p. 102.

19   See:

>   In them [the heavens] he has set a tent for the sun,
>   which comes out like a bridegroom leaving his chamber,
>   and, like a strong man, runs its course with joy. (Psalm 19:4-5)